Wines and Spirits

LOOKING BEHIND THE LABEL

Wines and Spirits

LOOKING BEHIND THE LABEL

Produced and published by the
Wine & Spirit Education Trust

WINE & SPIRIT EDUCATION TRUST ®

Wine & Spirit Education Trust
39–45 Bermondsey Street, London SE1 3XF
e-mail: wset@wset.co.uk
internet: www.WSETglobal.com

First published 2005
Fully revised edition 2014

A CIP catalogue record for this book is available from the British Library
ISBN 978 1 905819 25 6

PHOTOGRAPHIC CREDITS
2, 23, 69 (top), 71 (middle), 72 (Rob Lawson); 33, 41 (Sopexa); 37 (Kevin Judd); 44 (Weingut Reuscher-Haart); 59 (CIVB); 63 (González Byass); 64 (AICEP Portugal); 70 (Diageo); 71 (top) (Tomas Estes); 71 (bottom) (Adnams).

WSET: 6 (Karen Douglas); 9, 26, 29, 49, 51, 58 (Antony Moss); 13, 54 (Michael Buriak); 22 (Nicola Littlewood); 47 (Jude Mullins); 57 (Harriet Furze); 69 (bottom) (Erica Dent).

COVER PICTURES
Background: Victoria Clare
Top: Michael Buriak
Middle: Antony Moss
Bottom: The Dalmore Distillery

LABELS
Direct Wines Ltd: 16 (top right), 27 (top), 28, 31, 34 (middle right), 37 (top), 38, 42, 49 (bottom), 50, 56, 61

16 (middle left), 17 (bottom right), 26 (Constellation Brands); 16 (bottom right), 45 (ABS Wine Agencies); 17 (top right) (Casa Silva); 17 (middle left) (Domaine Huet); 27 (bottom) (Moët Hennessy UK Ltd); 27 (middle) (Chanson); 30 (Louis Jadot); 34 (top right, middle left, bottom left), 60 (bottom) (Union des Grands Crus de Bordeaux); 35 (Frog's Leap); 37 (middle) (Brancott Estate); 40 (Vidal-Fleury); 41 (Hecht & Bannier); 44 (Hugel); 46 (Liberty Wines); 48 (Montes); 49 (middle) (Domaines Schlumberger); 52 (C.V.N.E.); 53 (Castelgreve); 55 (Vino del Sol); 57 (top) (Graham Beck); 57 (middle) (Pol Roger UK); 57 (bottom) (Freixenet); 60 (top) (Domdechant Werner); 62 (González Byass); 63, 64 (John E Fells & Sons Ltd).

MAPS
Maps designed by Cosmographics Ltd

DIAGRAMS
Diagrams produced by CallowCraddock Ltd

Designed by Peter Dolton
Editing and proofreading by Cambridge Editorial Partnership Ltd
Production services by Wayment Print & Publishing Solutions Ltd
Printed and bound by Pureprint, Uckfield, UK

Contents

Introduction

Welcome to *Wines and Spirits: Looking Behind the Label*.

It is impossible to tell what a wine will taste like simply from the label – however, it is possible to know what the wine *should* taste like, and this is what this book seeks to address. *Looking Behind the Label* takes as a starting point the most prominent informative words appearing on the label of a bottle of wine. This could be a grape variety, or it could be a region – these are very powerful indicators of style.

Although there are some significant changes to this new edition of the book, much remains the same. To keep things as simple as possible, we continue to focus on the grape varieties and regions that are most frequently encountered – so please excuse us if the more obscure wines are not mentioned. Similarly, you will not find specific information about producers, brands and vintages.

The most important change has been made to the text itself, which has been reordered so that the focus throughout the sections on wine remains squarely on grape varieties. All the maps and the diagrams are completely new and, for the very first time, we include a fold-out global map at the back of the book. Together, all these changes have given us the space to introduce more labels in dedicated sections that focus on important labelling terms common to individual countries, regions or grape varieties.

So, for those readers who are taking the *WSET® Level 2 Award in Wines and Spirits*, I wish you every success in the examination. For those who are not, why not visit our website at www.WSETglobal.com for details of courses that are available throughout the world.

I do hope that you enjoy reading this book. If you wish to gain more in-depth knowledge of the wines and spirits of the world, I would recommend that you progress to the *WSET® Level 3 Award in Wines and Spirits* and its accompanying textbook *Wines and Spirits: Understanding Style and Quality*.

Ian Harris
Chief Executive, Wine & Spirit Education Trust

Tasting and Evaluating Wine

1

Tasting wine rather than simply drinking it increases our appreciation of the wine by allowing us to examine it in detail. Although the process can seem repetitive at first, with practice it becomes a subconscious habit.

The act of putting our sensations into words means the impression of the wine lingers longer in our memory. It also helps us communicate to other people what the wine is like, sometimes long after we have tasted it. This is an essential skill for anyone involved in the production, distribution or sale of wine. As we will see in Chapter 2, the successful pairing of food and wine requires us to consider the separate components of the wine. The WSET systematic approach to tasting, outlined below, shows us how to do this.

PREPARATION FOR TASTING

It is important that our impression of the wine is not altered by any outside influences. The ideal tasting room will be odour-free (no smells of cleaning products, tobacco, food or perfume), with good natural light, and white surfaces against which we can judge the appearance of our wines. Our tasting palate should be clean, and unaffected by tobacco, food, coffee, gum or toothpaste. Chewing a piece of bread can help remove any lingering flavours. Hayfever, colds and fatigue affect our ability to judge wines, because they affect our senses of taste and smell.

Many glasses have been developed to show different wines at their best. However, in order to make fair comparisons between wines, we need to use the same type of glass. At the WSET, we use the ISO glass, as illustrated on page 2. It has a rounded bowl that is large enough to swirl the wine. The sides slope inwards in a tulip shape to concentrate the aromas, and the stem allows us to hold the glass without warming the wine.

THE WSET LEVEL 2 SYSTEMATIC APPROACH TO TASTING WINE®

This approach methodically describes the different aspects of a wine in the order in which we encounter them. Appearance first, then the nose, then the palate, and finally we may use our impressions to draw a conclusion about the quality of the wine.

Appearance

The main reason for looking at the appearance of a wine is that it can warn us of faults. If a wine is too old, has been badly stored, or the cork seal has failed, allowing air to damage the wine, then it is described as out-of-condition. This is the most common fault that shows itself in the appearance: out-of-condition wines will be dull in appearance, and will have at least a hint of brown, although a brown colour does not always indicate a faulty wine. (Brown hints can appear in healthy old wines, particularly those that have been aged for very long periods in oak.) Haziness may indicate a fault, or it could be that the wine has deliberately not been filtered before bottling (see Chapter 4).

It is worth making a quick note of the colour. Look at the intensity: is it particularly intense or pale? If it is a red wine, is it ruby (purply-red) or garnet (orangey-red)? Purple is an indication of youth. Wines with a dominant purple colour will be called purple. Orange, amber and brown colours are indicators of age. Wines that are more dominant in these colours, rather than red, will be called tawny. However, bear in mind that some wines change colour more rapidly than others, so no definitive conclusions about actual age can be reached. If it is a white wine, is it lemon (yellow with a hint of green) or gold (yellow with a hint of orange)? Green indicates youth; orange and brown indicate age. For rosé wines, a bright purply-pink indicates youth; orange and brown hints indicate age.

The colour of a wine from any particular region or grape variety depends greatly on the age of the wine, and the winemaking techniques used. As it is impossible to generalise about the appearance of these wines, the descriptions throughout the book limit themselves to describing wines as red, rosé or white, with very few exceptions. The following are examples of more precise descriptions of appearance:

- clear, deep ruby
- clear, medium-intensity, garnet
- clear, pale gold
- hazy, dark brown.

(The last wine would almost certainly be faulty.)

Nose

The next step is to smell the wine. Swirl it in the glass to release as many aromas as possible, then take a sniff. Make a note of the **condition** of the nose. Are there any off-notes? The most common fault that can be discovered on the nose is cork taint. At low levels, this can strip the wine of its fresh, fruity aromas. At its worst, it can add a pungent, unpleasant damp cardboard or musty smell to the wine. Out-of-condition wines will smell dull and stale, and may have excessive oxidative aromas (toffee, caramel or sherry). However, the presence of oxidative aromas does not always indicate

the leather, the bread and so on. Make your aroma-description vocabulary as wide and precise as possible. Always be aware, however, that one purpose of a tasting note is to help describe a wine to someone who has not tasted it. Terms such as 'the back of my garage' or 'the glue we used to use at school', while useful for a private tasting notebook, are unlikely to help describe the wine to many other people.

Palate

It is often said that tasting is an entirely subjective matter. It is true that our sensitivities to sweetness, acidity, tannins and certain aroma compounds differ. Therefore our private experience of tasting the wines may be entirely different. However, even if we have different sensitivities to the components in a wine, we can usually agree which of any pair of wines is sweeter, more acidic, or more tannic. From this, it is a short step (although it requires a lot of tasting experience) before we can say whether a wine has medium, or particularly high or low levels of these components.

When assessing a wine on the palate you use your sense of taste (for sugar, acid and bitterness) and smell (for flavour characteristics). All parts of the tongue are sensitive to all tastes, but some areas are more sensitive than others. The exact pattern of sensitivities varies from taster to taster, but, generally, sweetness is most easily detected on the tip of the tongue, acidity at the sides and bitterness at the back. To ensure you gain the clearest possible impression of the wine, take a small tasting sip, then draw in air through your lips. This will ensure that the wine coats all parts of your mouth, and the vapours are carried up the back of your nose, where your sense of smell will detect the flavour character.

Sweetness is an indicator of how much sugar a wine contains, although wines made from very ripe grapes can have a slightly sweet flavour even when there is no sugar. Almost all red wines, and most white wines, are dry, that is, they contain almost no sugar. White wines that taste slightly sweet are described as 'off-dry'.

Acidity is what makes lemons taste sour. It causes the mouth to water, and its presence makes wines taste vibrant and refreshing. It is present in all wines, although levels in white wines are generally higher than acidity levels in reds. Certain varieties, such as Riesling and Sauvignon Blanc, give wines that are particularly high in acidity. Cool climates generally result in higher levels of acidity than hot climates. Acidity is very important for sweet wines. If it is too low, the wines taste oversweet, and cloying.

Tannin is what makes strong black tea taste bitter and astringent. Tannins are present in grape skins, and their presence in a wine depends on the amount of skin contact during winemaking (see Chapter 3). White and rosé wines receive very little, if any, skin contact, so

a fault: some wines, such as Oloroso Sherry (see Chapter 17), are deliberately oxidised during production. All faults can be detected on the palate too. When a fault is really bad it can be easily identified on the nose and the wine can be put to one side straightaway. However, in some cases when the fault is only minor, it is sometimes necessary to take a sip and assess the flavours on the palate in order to confirm that the wine is faulty.

Assuming the wine is healthy, how intense are the aromas? Are they particularly pronounced, or are they light and hard to detect? Describing the smell is a more subjective aspect. It will depend greatly on your previous experiences. Some of the descriptions may sound fanciful at first. However, there are well-understood reasons why aromas such as butter, vanilla, rose or raspberry appear in some wines. Other aromas are less well understood, but wine tasters can be quite consistent in their use. Some writers avoid using aroma descriptors, but in order to evoke the wine their tasting notes often use words such as 'feminine', 'elegant', 'clumsy'. These words can be very appropriate, but difficult to define. A more scientifically objective approach would involve naming the particular chemical compounds which are present, which is almost impossible to do accurately and would be useless to most wine drinkers!

On page 3 we have included a table of suggested aroma/flavour words, and how they might be grouped together. This is not an exhaustive list, but it is a very thorough starting point. We recommend that you taste the fruits, vegetables and spices, and smell the flowers, they rarely have any detectable tannin. Thick-skinned varieties (Cabernet Sauvignon, Syrah) have much higher tannin levels than thin-skinned ones (Pinot Noir, Grenache). High levels of soft ripe tannins may indicate a hot climate wine. Note that astringent tannins from unripe grapes can cause a strong, mouth-drying sensation, even when their levels are low. The bitter flavours are most strongly tasted at the back of the tongue; the astringent sensations are most strongly felt on the gums. Soft, ripe tannins contribute to the viscosity and body of the wine.

Body is also sometimes described as 'mouth-feel'. It is the sensation of richness, weight or viscosity, and is a combination of the effects of alcohol, tannins, sugars and flavour compounds extracted from the skins. It is possible for a wine such as Beaujolais to be high in alcohol (13% abv), but still be light in body because it has very little tannin, and is lightly flavoured.

In contrast to sweetness, acidity, tannins and body, which are detected in the mouth, **flavour characteristics** are detected when aroma components in the wine evaporate off the tongue and rise up to the back of the nose. This is why we cannot taste properly with a cold. To help these volatile flavour components reach the nose, many tasters slurp the wine by drawing air in through their lips while tasting it. The groups of flavour descriptors are the same as those for the nose.

The Finish refers to how long the desirable flavours linger in the mouth after the wine has been swallowed or spat out. A long, complex finish is an indicator of quality (see below).

Conclusions

Finally, having described our wine, we may form an assessment of its quality. A good starting point is to ask yourself whether you like the wine or not. If you like it, how much do you like it, and what do you like about it? If you did not enjoy it, try to articulate what you did not like about it.

Of course, an objective assessment of quality goes beyond personal likes and dislikes. You may dislike a particular wine because you do not like acidic or oaky wines, for example, but other wine consumers do like these styles. The key question is, is it a good example of its type? This question becomes easier to answer as you gain more experience. Assuming the wine is not faulty (badly made, out-of-condition, affected by cork taint), many criteria can differentiate between a poor wine, an acceptable wine and a great wine. These include:

Balance – Fruitiness and sweetness alone can make a wine taste sickly or cloying. Acidity and tannin alone or in excess can make a wine taste hard, unpleasant or austere. In a good quality wine, the sweetness and the fruitiness will be in balance with the tannin and acidity.

WSET LEVEL 2 SYSTEMATIC APPROACH TO TASTING WINE®

APPEARANCE		
Clarity		clear – hazy
Intensity		pale – medium – deep
Colour	white:	lemon – gold – amber
	rosé:	pink – salmon – orange
	red:	purple – ruby – garnet – tawny
NOSE		
Condition		clean – unclean
Intensity		light – medium – pronounced
Aroma characteristics		*e.g.* fruits, flowers, spices, vegetables, oak aromas, other
PALATE		
Sweetness		dry – off-dry – medium – sweet
Acidity		low – medium – high
Tannin		low – medium – high
Body		light – medium – full
Flavour characteristics		*e.g.* fruits, flowers, spices, vegetables, oak flavours, other
Finish		short – medium – long
CONCLUSIONS		
Quality		faulty – poor – acceptable – good – very good – outstanding

WSET Level 2 Wine-Lexicon:
supporting the WSET Level 2 Systematic Approach to Tasting Wine®

AROMA AND FLAVOUR CHARACTERISTICS	
FLORAL / FRUIT **Are the flavours simple/generic or specific? Fresh or cooked? Ripe or unripe?**	
Floral	blossom, rose, violet
Green Fruit	green apple, red apple, gooseberry, pear, grape
Citrus Fruit	grapefruit, lemon, lime (juice or zest?)
Stone Fruit	peach, apricot, nectarine
Tropical Fruit	banana, lychee, mango, melon, passion fruit, pineapple
Red Fruit	redcurrant, cranberry, raspberry, strawberry, red cherry, plum
Black Fruit	blackcurrant, blackberry, blueberry, black cherry
Dried Fruit	fig, prune, raisin, sultana, kirsch, jamminess, cooked, baked, stewed fruits, preserved fruits
SPICE / VEGETABLE	
Under-ripeness	green bell pepper (capsicum), grass, white pepper, leafiness, tomato, potato
Herbaceous	grass, asparagus, blackcurrant leaf
Herbal	eucalyptus, mint, medicinal, lavender, fennel, dill
Vegetable	cabbage, peas, beans, black olive, green olive
Sweet Spice	cinnamon, cloves, ginger, nutmeg, vanilla
Pungent Spice	black/white pepper, liquorice, juniper
OAK/OTHER	
Simplicity/Neutrality	simple, neutral, indistinct
Autolytic	yeast, biscuit, bread, toast, pastry, lees
Dairy	butter, cheese, cream, yoghurt
Oak	vanilla, toast, cedar, charred wood, smoke, resinous
Kernel	almond, coconut, hazelnut, walnut, chocolate, coffee
Animal	leather, meaty, farmyard
Maturity	vegetal, mushroom, hay, wet leaves, forest floor, game, savoury, tobacco, cedar, honey, cereal
Mineral	earth, petrol, rubber, tar, stony/steely, wet wool

Finish – A balanced, pleasant finish where the flavours linger for several seconds is an indicator of a high-quality wine. For inferior wines, the flavours may disappear almost instantly leaving no lingering impression, or the flavours that linger may be unpleasant.

Intensity – Dilute flavours can indicate a poor wine. However, extreme, intense flavours are not necessarily a sign of quality, because they can easily upset the balance of a wine and make it difficult to drink.

Complexity – Lesser wines often have one or two simple flavours and quickly become boring. The greatest wines generally have many different flavours.

Expressiveness – Lesser wines taste as if they could come from anywhere and be made with any grape variety. Great wines express characteristics of their grape variety and/or their region of production (climate, soils, traditional winemaking techniques). In a few rare cases, the individual vineyard can be identified from the flavours of the wine.

Selecting and Recommending Wines

When choosing wines for an occasion, or making a recommendation, it is important to take into account the **tastes** and **preferences** of those who will be consuming the wine (and the price requirements of whoever is paying!). When catering for large numbers of people with diverse or unknown tastes, it is wise to avoid extreme styles of wines such as Alsace Gewurztraminer or Barolo, and it can be a good idea to offer alternatives (dry/medium, red/white/rosé). When matching a wine to an **occasion**, remember that apart from in exceptional circumstances, the wine should not be the centre of attention. However, it should be of an appropriate quality: for special occasions it can be a good idea to trade up to a premium-quality wine. However, very fine, rare, special bottles may be best saved for a modest occasion where they can be given the attention they deserve: they will make that occasion a special one. Food is an important consideration when selecting a wine for an occasion. Pairing wine with food is the subject of the next chapter.

Tips for how to serve wine and how much you may need to supply are given in Chapter 6.

Wine with Food

2

Food that is consumed with wine has an effect on the way a wine tastes, and wine can also have an effect on the taste of food. The purpose of food and wine pairing is to take advantage of these effects, so that ideally both the food and wine provide more pleasure than either would when consumed separately. Knowledge of these effects will also help avoid negative or unpleasant interactions.

In addition to understanding the basic taste interactions between food and wine, it is important to remember that people have different sensitivities to various flavour and aroma components, meaning that the same level of bitterness, for example, can affect one person much more strongly than another (this is different from a personal preference – some people like strong reactions while others find them unpleasant). Pairings should therefore take into account the preferences of the individual, as well as the basic interactions between food and wine.

PRIMARY FOOD AND WINE TASTE INTERACTIONS

When you place food in your mouth, your taste buds adapt so that the perception of levels of sugar, salt, acid, etc. of the next item to be tasted can be altered. An extreme example is when orange juice becomes unpleasantly acidic when consumed immediately after using toothpaste. In addition to this, some foods such as chocolate or thick creamy dishes can have a mouth-coating effect that impairs the sense of taste.

In simple terms there are two components in food (sweetness and umami) that tend to make wines taste 'harder' (more astringent and bitter, more acidic, less sweet and less fruity), and two components (salt and acid) whose presence in food tends to make wines taste 'softer' (less astringent and bitter, less acidic, sweeter, and more fruity). Generally, food has more impact on the way a wine will taste than the other way round, and in particular is more likely to have a negative impact.

Sweetness in Food:
- Increases the perception of bitterness, acidity and the burning effect of the alcohol in the wine
- Decreases the perception of body, sweetness, and fruitiness in the wine

Sweetness in a dish can make a dry wine seem to lose its fruit and be unpleasantly acidic. With any dishes containing sugar, a good general rule is to select a wine that has a higher level of sweetness.

Umami in Food:
- Increases the perception of bitterness, acidity and alcohol burn in the wine
- Decreases the perception of body, sweetness and fruitiness in the wine

Umami is a savoury taste, and is distinct from the other primary tastes although it can be difficult to isolate. Whereas sweetness can be illustrated in isolation with sugar, salt with sodium chloride and acidity with a number of acids (e.g. tartaric acid), umami tends to be present with other tastes (with saltiness in Monosodium Glutamate (MSG)) or with other flavours (e.g. in cooked or dried mushrooms). One of the simplest ways to experience it is to compare the taste of a raw button mushroom with one that has been microwaved for 30 seconds. The umami taste of the mushroom is greatly increased by the cooking. Umami can also be experienced by tasting MSG – either by eating a few grains, or in a weak solution. Note, however, that in this form, the umami taste is combined with a salt taste.

Many foods that are considered difficult to pair contain high levels of umami without salt to counteract the hardening effects on wine. These include asparagus, eggs, mushrooms and ripe soft cheeses. Other foods that are high in umami also tend to be high in salt, which can counteract the impact of umami on the wine (see below). These include cured or smoked seafood and meats, and hard cheeses (especially Parmesan).

Acidity in Food:
- Increases the perception of body, sweetness and fruitiness in the wine
- Decreases the perception of acidity in the wine

Some acidity in food is generally a good thing for food and wine pairing as it can bring a very high acid wine into balance and enhance the fruitiness. However, if the level of acidity in the wine is low, high levels of acidity in foods can make wines seem flat, flabby and lacking focus.

Salt in Food:
- Increases the perception of body in the wine
- Decreases the perception of bitterness and acidity in the wine

Salt is another wine-friendly component of food which can help soften some of the harder elements.

Bitterness in Food:
- Increases bitterness in wine

Sensitivity to bitter tastes varies greatly from person to person. Generally, bitter flavours add to each other, so bitterness in the food alone may be at a pleasant level, and the bitterness in the wine may be balanced, but together the bitter elements can combine to reach an unpleasant level.

Chilli Heat in Food

This is a tactile (touch) sensation rather than one of taste and levels of sensitivity can vary greatly from person to person. Not only are some people more sensitive than others, but there is also huge variation in how pleasant or unpleasant this effect feels to the individual.

Chilli heat in food:
- Increases the perception of bitterness, acidity, and alcohol burn
- Decreases the perception of body, richness, sweetness and fruitiness in the wine

The intensity of the reaction increases with the level of alcohol in the wine. Alcohol also increases the burning sensation of the chilli; some people enjoy this effect.

OTHER CONSIDERATIONS

Flavour Intensity: It is usually desirable for the flavour intensities of the food and wine to be matched so that one does not overpower the other. However, in some circumstances, an intensely flavoured food (such as a curry) can be successfully partnered with a lightly flavoured wine – such as a simple, unoaked, light white. Equally, some lightly flavoured desserts can be successfully partnered with intensely flavoured sweet wines.

Acid and Fat: Most people find the combination of acidic wines with fatty or oily foods to be very satisfying. The pairing provides a pleasant sensation of the acidic wine 'cutting through' the richness of the food, and cleaning up the palate. This is a subjective effect.

Sweet and Salty: Also subjective is the pleasure of combining sweet and salty flavours, but this is a combination many people enjoy, and leads to some very successful food and wine pairings, such as sweet wine and blue cheese.

APPLYING THE PRINCIPLES

Because people vary in their sensitivities and preferences, there is no simple answer to the questions about which wines go best with which dishes and the host or sommelier should accept that their guests may not agree about which pairings work.

When selecting wines to partner dishes it can be helpful to divide dishes and wines into high risk and low risk. Of course, most foods and wines contain more than one of the structural components listed below so there are many possible permutations.

High-Risk Foods
- **Sugar** – dishes high in sugar should be paired with a wine that has at least as much sugar.
- **Umami** – dishes high in umami should be paired with wines that are more fruity than tannic as the umami in the food will emphasise the bitterness of the tannins.
- **Umami** – high levels of umami in a dish can be balanced by the addition of acid or salt. However, the amount added should not alter the basic character of the dish.
- **Bitterness** – dishes high in bitterness will emphasise bitterness in wine. Consider white wines or low-tannin reds.
- **Chilli heat** – dishes high in chilli heat should be paired with white wines or low-tannin reds, both with low alcohol (as bitterness and alcohol burn can be highlighted for sensitive tasters). Fruitiness and sweetness can also be reduced so think about wines

with higher levels of these qualities to mitigate this effect.

Low-Risk Foods – dishes high in **salt** and/or **acid**. Note, however:

- High-acid foods should generally be matched with high-acid wines, otherwise the wines can taste too soft and flabby.

High-Risk Wines

The more structural components in the wine (and food), the more possible taste interactions there will be. This makes pairing more complicated but also provides potential for more interesting results. The most problematic wines are those that have high levels of bitterness from oak and skin tannins, combined with high levels of acidity and alcohol, and complex flavours. However, these wines can undergo the most interesting changes when partnered with food and can reveal flavours that are hard to detect when the wines are consumed on their own.

Low-Risk Wines

Simple, unoaked wines with a little residual sugar are unlikely to be made unpleasant by any dishes. However, these kinds of wines change relatively little when partnered with food, so the food and wine pairing experiences can be less interesting.

One of the most productive ways of applying the principles identified above is to examine well-established successful pairings, and analyse the reasons for the success. If these reasons are understood, then other wines can be identified that can also provide successful pairings. For example, Champagne works well with oysters because it is unoaked (so there is no bitter component to be spoiled by the umami taste of the oyster), relatively light in flavour (so as not to overwhelm the delicate flavour of oysters) and high in acid (so it still seems vibrant and refreshing when oysters are eaten with lemon juice, for example). Other wines that satisfy these criteria should also be successful pairings.

3 Factors Affecting Wine Style, Quality and Price

Wine is made from the fruit of the grape vine.

The main factors that determine how a wine will taste are: the grape variety used; the environment in which it is grown (climate and weather, soil and slope); the care with which the grapes are grown and harvested; how the wine is made; and how it is matured (including bottle-age). Many of the factors that affect quality have a cost effect and will influence the final selling price of a bottle of wine.

GRAPE VARIETY

Just as there are different kinds of apples and potatoes, there are different varieties of grapes. Over centuries, particular vines have been chosen that have desirable characteristics (pleasant flavour, high yields, and resistance to disease and so on). These chosen vines include those that are most well known to us, such as Chardonnay and Cabernet Sauvignon, as well as many hundreds of others. The type of grape used determines a large part of the character of the wine: as well as affecting the flavours and colour of the wine, different grape varieties have different levels of sugar (for alcohol), acidity and tannins. The particular characteristics of different major grape varieties are discussed in the sections covering those varieties. Not all Chardonnays, or Cabernet Sauvignons, taste the same or cost the same. This is because the other factors have an important effect on style and quality.

ENVIRONMENT

In order to grow and produce a crop of ripe, healthy grapes, a vine needs **carbon dioxide** (CO_2), **sunlight**, **water**, **warmth** and **nutrients**. The first of these is found in the air (much of it is breathed out by animals), but the availability of the other four is affected by the vine's environment. In particular, climate and weather affect sunlight, heat and water, and the soil affects warmth and water, as well as the availability of nutrients.

Climate

Climate describes what weather conditions (temperatures, rainfall, sunshine) we may expect in a typical year. Climates suitable for wine production can be divided into three categories; hot, moderate and cool. Broadly speaking, the climate of a wine region is determined by latitude or, in other words, how close it is to the Equator. The closer a region is to the Equator, the hotter it is. For example, South Africa has a hotter climate than Germany. However, there are two other important factors to consider: altitude and the oceans. A region that is at a high altitude will have a cooler climate than a region closer to sea level, even if they share the same latitude. The influence the ocean has on a wine region depends on the temperature of the water. There is a warm ocean current that ensures that Western Europe is not as cold as regions with a similar latitude in North America. Conversely, many of the wine regions of California, Chile and South Africa are cooled by cold ocean currents.

The climate type can have a dramatic effect on the flavour of ripe grapes. Some grape varieties (such as Cabernet Sauvignon) need a lot of heat to ripen fully. If the grapes have not fully ripened, wines from these varieties will taste excessively sour, astringent, bitter and lacking in fruit flavours. Other grapes (such as Sauvignon Blanc and Pinot Noir) need a moderate or cool climate otherwise they over-ripen and lose their refreshing fruit character and acidity. Unpleasant jammy or raisiny cooked flavours may then dominate the wine, or it may simply taste bland. A few grapes (such as Chardonnay) can make interesting wines in hot, moderate and cool climates.

The flavours in the wine give clues as to the climate; and there are more details on how climate affects the flavour and style of wines in the separate grape variety chapters. In general, we may say that:

- hot climate: more alcohol, fuller body, more tannin, less acidity
- cool climate: less alcohol, lighter body, less tannin, more acidity.

Weather

As weather conditions vary from one year to the next, the weather of each particular year affects the style and quality of wines from that year. The most important time is the growing season, particularly when the grapes are ripening. Extreme weather conditions such as hail, high winds, floods and late frosts can cause problems with the size and quality of the crop. Hail in particular can cause a great deal of damage to ripening grapes and to vines. Once the skins of grapes have been damaged, they are very susceptible to rot. Unusually cool or hot weather can affect the style and quality of the wines produced in a given year (vintage). Vintages are most important in regions such as Bordeaux and Champagne, where the weather varies greatly from one year to the next. Modern grape growing and winemaking techniques mean that even in these regions, differences between vintages are becoming less pronounced, and there are fewer bad years. Blending of varieties, or between different sites, villages or even regions, is a useful way to keep style and quality consistent from one year to the next. This is especially important for branded wines.

Sunlight

Sunlight is the source of the energy that allows the grape to combine carbon dioxide and water into sugar. From a winemaking perspective, these sugars are the most important part of a grape for it is these that are fermented to become alcohol. Quite simply, without sunlight, carbon dioxide and water, there would be no grape sugars; and without grape sugars there would be no wine. In regions far away from the Equator, vines can receive more sunlight by being planted on slopes that angle them towards the sun, or above rivers that reflect sunlight. In sunny regions, this is unnecessary.

Water

Water can come from rain, or from the ground, or from irrigation. Too much water can cause grapes to become bloated. This may result in bigger crops, but the flavours and sugars will be diluted, and the wine will have less alcohol, body and flavour. In areas where rainfall is high, such as much of Europe, the best vineyards are on slopes or soils, such as gravel or chalk, which drain water away quickly. In regions where there is insufficient rainfall, such as many parts of the New World, irrigation is essential if the vine is to survive. For the highest quality wines, just enough water is provided to sustain sugar production. For cheaper wines, irrigation can be used to increase the size of the crop. Although a supply of water is essential for wine production, too much rain can cause problems, with wet conditions encouraging the growth of rot. Rain and hail can damage vines and grapes.

Warmth

Warmth is needed for the production of sugars – but not too little or too much. If the weather is too cool or too hot, sugar production slows and can stop. This is one of the reasons why most of the world's vineyards are found in a temperate zone between 30° and 50° from the Equator. A vine can keep itself cool by evaporating water through its leaves. This process occurs more rapidly in hot, dry, conditions. In extreme cases, the vine may shut down its leaves to prevent the plant drying out, so, although there is warmth and heat, no sugars are produced. The main factors affecting warmth are climate and weather. In addition, soils vary in their ability to absorb or reflect warmth. Dry, stony soils are generally warmer than wet clay soils, for example.

Nutrients

The sugars produced by the leaves do not just provide sweetness in the grapes, they are also the building blocks for the whole vine. In a sense, almost the entire plant is built out of the material provided by the carbon dioxide in the air, and the water obtained via its roots.

MAIN EFFECTS ON CLIMATE		
Latitude	Closer to the Equator e.g. Australia, South Africa	Hotter
	Further from the Equator e.g. Germany, New Zealand South Island	Cooler
Altitude	Higher e.g. the best areas of Argentina	Cooler
The sea	Warm ocean currents e.g. Western Europe	Hotter
	Cold ocean currents e.g. California, Chile, the South African Cape, Southern Australia	Cooler
Regions in the centre of large land masses (e.g. Burgundy, central Spain) have hotter summers and colder winters than regions near the coast (e.g. Bordeaux).		

However, the plant also needs tiny amounts of nutrients, in the right balance. These are provided by the soil. Grapevines are very tolerant, and will grow in a wide range of soils. In general, provided there are sufficient nutrients, poorer soils result in better quality grapes.

GRAPE GROWING

Over the course of the vineyard year, the two main factors that affect the quality and style of the raw grape material are the degree of care that is taken in the vineyard, and the control of the yields.

There are many **vineyard activities** that can help all the grapes to ripen fully, at the same time. These include careful pruning, controlling the number of bunches of grapes on each vine, and the careful positioning of the leaves to increase or lower the temperature of the grape bunches, or their degree of exposure to sunlight. These techniques all use expensive labour, which increases the cost as well as the quality. The other options are minimal pruning and maximum mechanisation, which

Both black and white grapes have the same bright green colour prior to ripening.

Cross-section of a grape berry

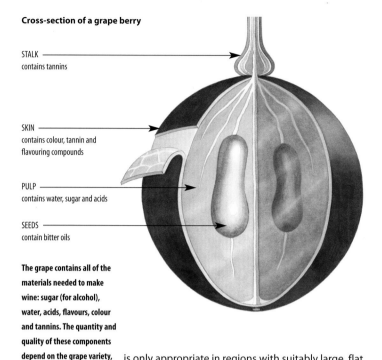

STALK
contains tannins

SKIN
contains colour, tannin and
flavouring compounds

PULP
contains water, sugar and acids

SEEDS
contain bitter oils

The grape contains all of the
materials needed to make
wine: sugar (for alcohol),
water, acids, flavours, colour
and tannins. The quantity and
quality of these components
depend on the grape variety,
the environment where it has
ripened, and how it has been
grown.

is only appropriate in regions with suitably large, flat
vineyards.

Yields also have an effect on quality. Lower yields
generally result in riper grapes with more concentrated
flavours, but controlling yields by limiting the number
of grape bunches takes time. Also, because the crop is
smaller, each kilogram costs more to grow and will have
to sell for a higher price if the effort is to be worthwhile.
The other option is to maximise yields using irrigation to
fill the grapes with water, with the result that flavours
and sugars are diluted. The resulting wine will be cheap,
but probably not very interesting. Most wines lie
somewhere between these two extremes.

In addition to the effects of soil, slope, climate,
weather, and care in the vineyard, some **pests and
diseases** are bad for the production of healthy grapes:

- Animal pests (including birds and insects) can damage
  shoots, buds, leaves, and may eat the grapes.
- Attacks of fungal diseases such as mildew or rot can
  damage green parts of the vine as well as leading to
  spoiled grapes.
- Long-term diseases caused by fungi, bacteria or
  viruses can affect the health of the vine, reducing
  yields and inhibiting ripening. Some eventually lead
  to the death of the vine.

The **harvest** occurs once the grapes have ripened. In
larger vineyards on flatter sites, harvesting will generally
be done by machines which shake the grapes off their
stems. Where whole bunches of grapes are needed, the
grapes must be hand-harvested. Steep sites with difficult
access must also be hand-harvested, and regions where
labour is cheap may hand-harvest, even where machines
could be used. Top-quality wines can be made from
both machine-harvested and hand-harvested grapes.

WINEMAKING

The most important part of this process is fermentation.
When yeasts feed on sugars in the grape juice, they
produce alcohol, carbon dioxide and heat, changing the
flavours of the grape juice into those of wine.

The flesh of almost all wine grape varieties is white.
The colour of red and rosé wines is obtained by soaking
the coloured skins in the fermenting juice. If the skins are
removed at an early stage, there is little or no colour. This
is how rosé wines are made from black grapes. White
wine can be made from black or white grapes. Red wine
can only be made from black grapes.

White Wines

For white wines, the grapes are usually **crushed** to break
the skins before they are **pressed** to separate out the
juice. Yeast is added. This will usually be a commercially
obtained yeast culture, which gives predictable results.
Some winemakers choose not to use commercial yeasts,
believing that the 'natural' yeasts that dwell in the
vineyard and winery give more interesting results.

The must is transferred to a **fermentation** vessel
(usually a stainless steel tank, but some winemakers use
oak barrels or open-topped concrete or wooden
fermenters). White wines are then fermented at low
temperatures (typically 12°C–22°C), to preserve delicate
fruit aromas. This takes between two and four weeks.

Sweetness in white wines is caused by unfermented
sugar. Sweet wines are discussed in Chapter 16.

Red Wines

Black grapes for red wines are **crushed** to release the
juice, then the juice and skins are put in the fermenting
vessel together. **Fermentation** takes place at a higher
temperature for red than for white wine (20°C–32°C).
Alcohol helps the **extraction** of colour, tannins and
flavours from the skins. In order to keep the juice in
contact with the skin, the juice may be pumped over the
floating skins or the skins may be 'punched down' into
the juice. The amount of colour and tannin in the
finished wine depends on how long the wine is kept in
contact with the skins. This may be for more than two
weeks for richly flavoured wines such as top-quality
Bordeaux, or as little as five days for light wines such as
Beaujolais. It also depends on how much tannin, colour
and flavour is in the skins – some black grape varieties
are naturally light in colour and tannins. Hot climates
encourage higher colour and tannin levels in the grapes.

When enough colour and tannin have been extracted,
the free run wine is drawn off. The skins are then **pressed**,
yielding a further quantity of wine, known as the 'press
wine'. Press wines contain higher levels of tannin, and
may be blended with free run wine to produce the style
required.

Rosé Wines

Like red wines, rosé wines must be made from black
grapes. The method of production is similar to that for

red wines, but they are fermented at a lower temperature (12°C–22°C). They must also have a much shorter period of grapeskin contact (12 to 36 hours). Pink wines labelled as 'white' Zinfandel are made this way.

Oak Flavours

Many wines receive some oak contact, often in the form of staves (small planks) or chips (large splinters) added to a vat. Extra money pays for better quality staves or chips. The very cheapest method of adding oak flavours is to use oak essence. In the finest wines all oak contact must be achieved by fermenting or ageing the wine in oak barrels. If a wine is fermented or aged in oak, a large premium has to be paid, particularly if the oak is new, because oak is expensive. French or European oak is more expensive than American oak, but tends to give more subtle, toast and nutty flavours and smoother tannins, whereas the American oak gives sweet coconut and vanilla but harsher tannins. A further premium is also to be paid where the highest-quality air-dried staves and expert cooperage is sought. Looking after a wine in oak barrels, and ensuring it is always topped up to avoid air in the cask spoiling the wine, is labour-intensive and therefore expensive.

Fermentation, as well as ageing, in oak barrels is common for premium Chardonnay wines, including many of those made in Burgundy. It is impractical to ferment red wines in barrels, but many premium red wines are aged in oak.

MATURATION

Maturation can take place in barrels or large neutral wooden or stainless steel vats. It also takes place in the bottle after bottling. The most important changes that occur are the slow chemical reactions that can allow complex flavours to develop.

Maturation with Oxygen

We have already seen that new oak directly adds oaky flavours to the wine. Old oak vats do not directly add any flavours. However, in both cases, the vessel is porous and allows small amounts of oxygen to dissolve in the wine. This softens the tannins in red wines, making the wine taste smoother, and can cause flavours such as toffee, fig, nut (hazelnut, almond, walnut) and coffee to develop.

Maturation without Oxygen

Bottles, cement and stainless steel vats are airtight and do not add any flavours, and the chemical reactions that occur are different to those in oak. In large stainless steel vats, the wine flavours stay almost unchanged for months. Changes occur faster in bottles because they are smaller. In bottles, in the absence of oxygen, the fresh fruit aromas of young wines change into cooked fruit, vegetal and animal notes (wet leaves, mushroom, leather).

Few wines improve in the bottle. It is common for the attractive fruit flavours simply to fade away, and nothing else to appear in their place. Often the animal and

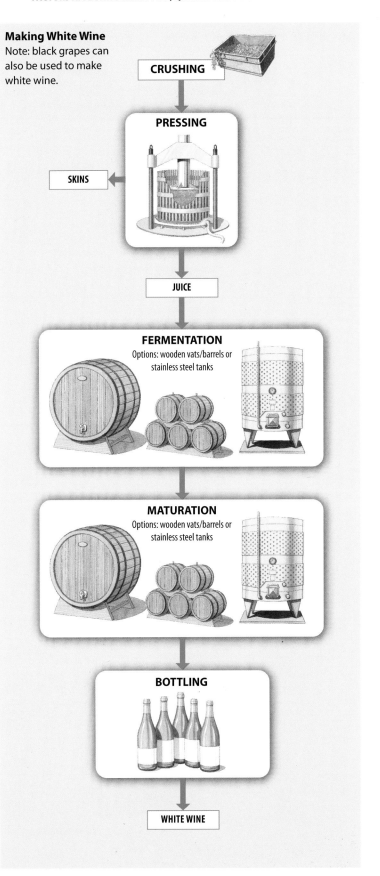

Making White Wine
Note: black grapes can also be used to make white wine.

CRUSHING

PRESSING

SKINS

JUICE

FERMENTATION
Options: wooden vats/barrels or stainless steel tanks

MATURATION
Options: wooden vats/barrels or stainless steel tanks

BOTTLING

WHITE WINE

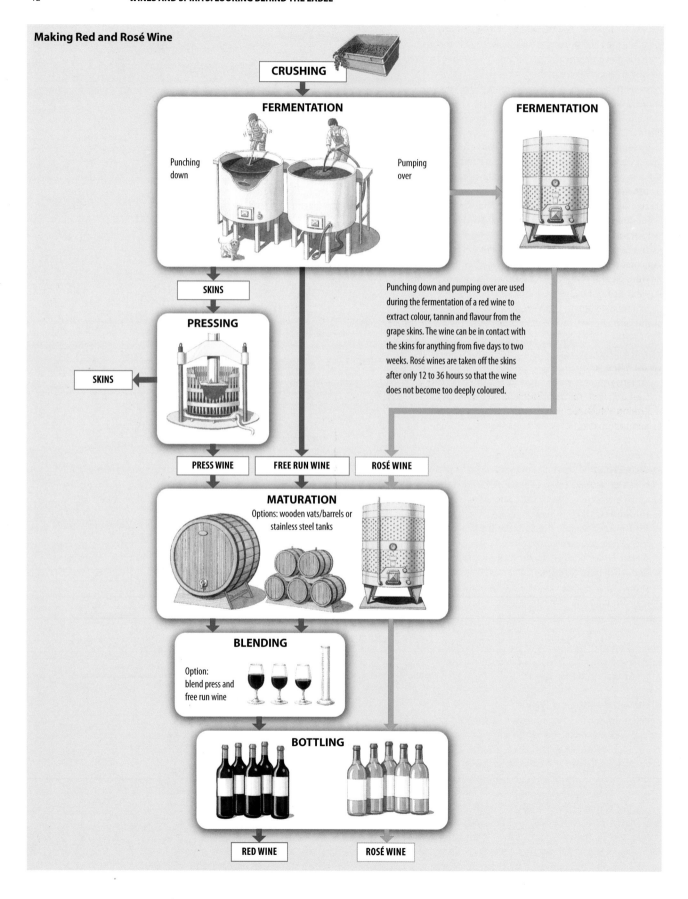

vegetal notes that develop will be unpleasant. For a few special wines, the fruit character remains while the other complex flavours develop around it. These wines are not easy to make, and are usually expensive to buy, but the flavours they offer are among the most rewarding of all wines.

FACTORS AFFECTING COST

It is useful to summarise here some of the factors that affect the cost of producing a bottle of wine.

In the Vineyard

- Cost of vineyard land: sites with the greatest potential for quality can be vastly more expensive than ordinary locations.
- The degree to which the vineyard work is mechanised (almost impossible for very steep sites).
- The cost and availability of labour and/or equipment.
- Yield size and the degree of selection of grape material: discarding underripe or rotten grapes can be enormously labour intensive and, like yield control, must be justified in the final selling price.

In the Winery

- Winery equipment, and how efficiently this is used.
- Cost of barrels or other forms of oak flavouring.
- Ageing, which requires expensive storage facilities and ties up capital.

Packaging, Distribution and Sale

- Exchange rates can affect the final selling price for exported bottles.
- Packaging (bottles, etc.) and cartons for distribution. Unusual bottles cost extra.
- Transport costs (these are a surprisingly small part of the selling price of most wines: shipping long distances by sea is relatively inexpensive).
- The efficiency of the distributor and retailer, and the profit margins they expect. Low-volume, high-service distribution costs more.

Bunches of ripe Barbera grapes in Alba.

Taxes and levies are also absorbed in the final retail price of a bottle of wine.

The ultimate factor that determines the selling price of a bottle of wine is how much the consumer is willing to pay. A bottle may be very expensive to produce, but if the quality does not match the price it will not sell. Marketing and the reputations of the producers, regions or brands can help sustain high prices, but if the quality fails to match consumers' expectations, then they move on to other wines. The reason that some regions continue to sell their wines at extremely high prices is that there are people who are prepared to pay high prices for those levels of quality. If the market disappeared, then the prices of these wines would fall or they would no longer be made.

Throughout this book, a distinction is made between wines that are produced in large volumes and/or sold at inexpensive prices, and premium-quality wines, which are usually more expensive. Quality is discussed at the end of Chapter 1.

4 Understanding the Label

The most prominent pieces of information on most wine labels are usually the brand or producer, the country or region, and/or the variety of grape used to make the wine. Where a variety is not named, very often it can be deduced from the region (many European regions specify which grape varieties can be used. For example, a wine from the Chablis appellation has to be made with Chardonnay). Specific varieties and regions are covered in later chapters. This chapter will help you to understand the rest of the information found on the wine label.

PRODUCERS AND BRANDS

The name of the producer and/or the distributor will be found somewhere on the label. For some famous brands this will be the most important term. For other wines it will be hidden in the small print. Some brand names are created by or reflect the producer. These would include château or estate names, and large-scale brands such as Jacob's Creek and E & J Gallo. Others are created by distributors or retailers. These include buyer's-own-brands (BOBs), such as wines sold under the name of a supermarket.

Port, Sherry and sparkling wine are dominated by a small number of large brands. For many consumers, the names of many grape varieties (Chardonnay, Shiraz…) and regions (Chablis, Sancerre…) act just like brands: they help the consumer make a decision by creating expectations of what the wine will be like. If those expectations are positive ones, and if the wines continue to meet the consumers' expectations, then those words on the label will help sell the wine.

VINTAGE

A vintage is usually stated on the label. This is the year in which the grapes were harvested (see page 17). Most wines are best consumed while they are young and fresh, and should not be aged. For these wines, the vintage acts as an indication of how old the wine is. For a few prestigious, age-worthy wines, vintages make a huge difference. For example, the price and quality of a 2009 wine from a good Bordeaux estate will be much higher than that of their 2007 wine. This is because 2009 was an outstanding year with almost perfect weather, whereas 2007 was not and therefore the wines from this vintage are less complex and are unlikely to last as long.

Seasons in the northern and southern hemispheres are inverted and relative to each other. Wines from a given vintage are made from grapes harvested in February, March or April (southern hemisphere) and August, September or October (northern hemisphere). As a result, southern hemisphere wines will be half a year older than northern hemisphere wines from the same vintage. This can make a difference for wines that are made to be consumed as young and fresh as possible, such as rosés and fruity unoaked whites.

GEOGRAPHICAL INDICATIONS

Geographical indications (GI) are common to all wine regions and are a common feature on wine labels. This is because the area where grapes are grown has a defining influence on the style, quality and flavour of the wine. A GI is a designated vineyard area within a country. These areas can be very large and cover an entire region (e.g. Bordeaux) or they can be very small and be no more than a single vineyard. Understandably, the use of geographical indications is tightly controlled to ensure that the consumer gets what they are paying for and that the wine is made from the grapes grown in the location stated on the label. The rules and regulations are very complex but throughout the world, wine can be divided into two categories:
- wines with a GI
- wines without a GI.

European Union

The European Union (EU) wines with a geographical indication (GI) are divided into two quality categories: wines with a **Protected Designation of Origin** (**PDO**), and wines with a **Protected Geographical Indication** (**PGI**). Although these are label terms they rarely appear on the label. Instead, producers use long-established traditional labelling terms, such as Appellation d'Origine Contrôlée in France. Broadly speaking, PDOs are smaller areas with more tightly defined regulations, whereas PGIs are larger with fewer regulations.

Importantly, these GIs not only define the geographical area of a region but also specify permitted vinegrowing and winemaking techniques and grape varieties. Therefore, in theory, each PDO has a unique flavour that cannot be copied by any other wine because the wine must be made according to the laws that specify: the limits of the area, the permitted vinegrowing and winemaking techniques, and the permitted grape varieties. PDO wines rarely state the grape variety on the label. This can mean that some of the finest expressions of Chardonnay, for example, come in bottles labelled as Chablis AC or Meursault AC.

Because the laws for producing PDOs are restrictive, some producers prefer to make wines in the PGI category because it allows the use of non-traditional varieties in the blend (e.g. Chardonnay in the south of France). These produce large quantities of inexpensive wines from international grape varieties such as Chardonnay, Sauvignon Blanc, Cabernet Sauvignon, Merlot and Syrah. The variety or blend is usually stated on the label. Where no varieties are mentioned, the wine is more likely to be made from lesser-known, local grape varieties.

Wine without a GI is the category that offers the most flexible production rules. For example, it allows brand owners to source grapes from vineyards throughout a country.

France – In France, the traditional labelling term for PDO is **Appellation d'Origine Contrôlée** (**AC** or **AOC**). The traditional labelling term for PGI wines is **Vin de Pays** (**VdP**). However, some of these regions (in particular the **Pays d'Oc**) prefer not to use VdP and choose instead to use the French for PGI, **Indication Géographique Protégée** (**IGP**). Wines without a geographical indication are labelled as **Vin de France**.

Italy – In Italy there are two traditional labelling terms that are used instead of PDO. The most important, used by only a select number of regions, is **Denominazione di Origine Controllata e Garantita** (**DOCG**). The other is **Denominazione di Origine Controllata** (**DOC**). The Italian labelling term for PGI is traditionally referred to as **Indicazione Geografica Tipica** (**IGT**). This is equivalent to the French's *Vin de Pays*. Some IGTs are vast and widely used (e.g. IGT Sicilia) and others are seldom seen.

Spain – Spain has several traditional labelling terms for PDO. Two are more widely used than the rest. The most prestigious, used by only two regions, is **Denominación de Origen Calificada** (**DOCa**). The other is **Denominación de Origen** (**DO**). The traditional Spanish labelling term for PGI is **Vino de la Tierra** (**VdlT**).

Germany – Germany also has two traditional labelling terms that they use instead of PDO: **Qualitätswein** and **Prädikatswein**. However, unlike Spain and Italy, these labelling terms are not used to denote a quality hierarchy. Wines that are labelled under these categories must be produced within one of Germany's 13 designated wine regions. However, wines labelled *Prädikatswein* are subdivided into six sub-categories

that are defined by the sugar level of the grapes at harvest. The traditional labelling term for PGI in Germany is *Landwein*, although the PGI category is not as widely used in Germany as it is in France, Italy and Spain.

New World
Nearly all non-EU wines in the international market fall into the category of 'Wines with a GI'. Each country has developed its own way of dividing its GI vineyard areas (whether it be by political boundaries or other specific areas, such as regions, zones, districts, and so on), and each control the use of their names. However, unlike in the EU, these legal categories are rarely seen on the label.

LEGALLY DEFINED QUALITY INDICATIONS
As well as PDOs and PGIs, most EU countries have other labelling terms that indicate quality defined in their wine laws.

France – In France, most appellations are sub-divided into a quality hierarchy, with the most prestigious covering the smallest areas and having the strictest regulations. Many different labelling terms are used to indicate these hierarchies, including **Villages**, **Premier Cru** and **Grand Cru**. Each of the major wine regions in France use these terms slightly differently. These individual regulations are covered throughout Chapters 7 to 14.

Italy – In Italy there are two important labelling terms that appear on many Italian wine labels: **Classico** and **Riserva**. These are discussed in more detail in Chapter 14.

Spain – The wine laws in Spain define specific ageing criteria for Spanish wines. Each category is defined by the minimum length of time the wine must be aged, both in barrel and in bottle, before it can be released for sale. Because these vary from one region to another, they are often exceeded by producers. This period of ageing can have a significant impact on the style and quality of a wine. In order of increasing minimum age, they are: **Joven**, **Crianza**, **Reserva** and **Gran Reserva**. These are discussed in more detail in Chapter 14.

Terminology for Geographical Indications in a selection of European languages

	Traditional terms for PDO wines	Traditional terms for PGI wines
France	Appellation d'Origine Contrôlée (AOC)	Vin de Pays (VdP)
Italy	Denominazione di Origine Controllata (DOC), Denominazione di Origine Controllata e Garantita (DOCG)	Indicazione Geografica Tipica (IGT)
Spain	Denominación de Origen (DO), Denominación de Origen Calificada (DOCa)	Vino de la Tierra (VdlT)
Germany	Prädikatswein, Qualitätswein	Landwein

READING THE LABEL

In these two pages we explore some of the common features found on wine labels throughout the world.

GEOGRAPHICAL INDICATIONS (GIs)

Nearly all wines have a GI. These can be small, such as Vouvray (LE MONT) and Stellenbosch (JORDAN), or much larger areas such as California (SIMPLY NAKED). However, typically only wines from the EU will show the legal classification of the GI. For LE MONT this is *Appellation Contrôlée*.

Some wines do not have a GI and CHANTE-CLAIR, a *Vin de France*, is one such example.

OAK

The role played by oak in the winemaking process is often indicated on the label. JORDAN says *barrel-fermented* and will show oak character, whereas SIMPLY NAKED is *unoaked* and will not.

COMMON LABELLING INFORMATION

1 Vintage: the year the grapes are harvested.

2 Alcohol: this is the alcoholic strength of the wine expressed as alcohol by volume (abv).

3 Volume: this is the amount of wine in the bottle. 750 mL or 75 cL is the size of a standard bottle.

NOTE: Producers often display this information on the back label as is the case with CHANTE-CLAIR.

This is used to indicate quality because old vines often produce better quality fruit.

This indicates that the wine is medium-dry.

SINGLE VARIETALS vs BLENDS

DOÑA DOMINGA and MENDOCINO VINEYARDS are both made using Chardonnay. Where MENDOCINO VINEYARDS is a single varietal wine, DOÑA DOMINGA is a blend of Chardonnay and Semillon, so both varietals appear on the label.

APPELLATION vs VARIETAL LABELLING

Both LE MONT and JORDAN are made from Chenin Blanc. However, the variety only appears on one (JORDAN). LE MONT uses an appellation on the label instead. Only by knowing the appellation of Vouvray would you know that it is made from 100 per cent Chenin Blanc.

This indicates that the grapes were grown without the use of synthetic chemicals.

Germany – Within the *Prädikatswein* category, there is a hierarchy of designations that is defined by the sugar level content of the grapes at the time of harvest. These are divided into six sub-categories. In order of minimum sugar level, from lowest to highest, they are: **Kabinett, Spätlese, Auslese, BA (Beerenauslese), Eiswein** and **TBA (Trockenbeerenauslese)**. These categories can apply to all grape varieties, though the best examples are made with Riesling. More detail on the styles of these wines can be found in Chapters 12 and 16.

A common misconception is that whereas EU wine production is closely regulated, in other countries producers are free to do what they like. It is true that outside PDO wine production, producers have more freedom to experiment with vinegrowing and winemaking techniques such as irrigation and oak chips, and have more choice over which varieties to plant and where to grow them. However, all countries have their own legislation covering production techniques and use of labelling terms to prevent consumers from being misinformed or, worse, harming their health. In addition, any wine that is imported into the EU has to satisfy EU laws covering wine-production techniques.

STYLE AND PRODUCTION TECHNIQUES

Apart from the variety, the region and the brand, the most common terms found on wine labels are indications of style or production techniques. Those in English, such as 'hand-harvested', 'unoaked' or 'estate-bottled' are often self-explanatory. But some may need a little further clarification. For wine produced in countries where English is not the first language, many common labelling terms are simply translations of words such as 'red wine', 'medium-dry', and so on. A table of these common terms can be found below.

Barrel/barrique-fermented (white wines only) – Fermenting the wine in oak gives a better integration of oak flavours in the wine, but it is more labour-intensive than simply ageing in oak, and therefore more expensive.

Barrel/barrique-aged – Many wines are aged in oak barrels or barrique prior to bottling. New oak barrels give a wine more oak flavours than used ones do. Therefore if the label states that the barrels are 'new' the wine will have a pronounced oak flavour (see Chapter 3).

Oaked – This indicates that the wine has been in contact with oak. This could be through ageing in oak vessels (of any size, new or old) during the maturation process. Alternatively, it could indicate the use of oak staves or chips (see Chapter 3). These last techniques would not be used for any premium-quality wines.

Unfined/Unfiltered – Most wines are treated before bottling to remove anything that may cause haziness. Some argue that one side effect of fining and/or filtration is that too much of the character of the wine is stripped away, so a few producers prefer to minimise or avoid clarifying their wines before bottling. They may indicate this by stating on the label that the wines are unfined and/or unfiltered. These wines are more likely to form deposits in the bottle as they age, and are less likely to be perfectly clear and bright in the glass.

***Botrytis cinerea*/Noble rot** – Botrytis is a fungus, or mould, that attacks grape berries. If it attacks healthy, ripe grapes it causes desirable noble rot used in the production of sweet wines. In other certain circumstances, however, it will form unwanted grey rot. More information on botrytis is provided in Chapter 16. Some producers will choose not to use the term *cinerea* on the label.

Organic – Wine made from grapes grown without the use of synthetic fertilisers, pesticides and herbicides are called 'organic'. Biodynamics is a system of organic grape growing and winemaking that links vineyard and winemaking activities to the positions of the moon, planets and stars.

Labelling terms in a selection of European languages

ENGLISH	FRENCH	ITALIAN	SPANISH	GERMAN
Wine	Vin	Vino	Vino	Wein
Red	Rouge	Rosso	Tinto	Rot
Rosé	Rosé	Rosato	Rosado	Rosé
White	Blanc	Bianco	Blanco	Weiss
Dry	Sec	Secco	Seco	Trocken
Medium-dry	Demi-sec	Abboccato	Semiseco	Halbtrocken
Medium-sweet	Moelleux	Amabile	Semidulce	Lieblich
Sweet	Doux	Dolce	Dulce	Süss
Vintage	Millésime	Annata	Añada/Cosecha	Jahrgang
Harvest	Vendange Récolte	Vendemmia	Vendimia	Ernte

Cuvée – This is a common labelling term widely used to indicate a specific blend or selection. It could be a blend of different varieties, regions, vintages, or even of different barrels or vats from the same estate or vineyard. It is often accompanied with a particular name. Producers often use this term to identify the better wines in their ranges. However, there are no legal controls on this term and therefore it cannot be taken as an indication of quality.

Old vines/*Vieilles vignes* – Old vines, or in French *vieilles vignes*, typically give lower yields of higher-quality grapes. This is not a legally defined term and as a result there can be some controversy over the use of this term.

An **Estate** (**Château**, **Domaine**) only uses grapes it has grown on its own land. A **Merchant**, or Négociant, blends together wines and/or grapes bought in from winemakers and grape farmers. The word 'Merchant', or 'Négociant' seldom appears on the bottle, but most medium and large-volume brands follow this model. A **co-operative cellar** (cave coopérative, cantina sociale) is a winemaking facility whose ownership is shared by a number of grape farmers.

5   Social Responsibility

Alcohol is an integral ingredient of wine, contributing to its structure and the flavour. However, alcohol is an addictive substance which, if consumed to excess, can have damaging consequence for one's health, happiness and financial security.

ALCOHOL LEGISLATION

Because of the harmful effects of excessive alcohol consumption, most countries have legislation to control its misuse. The legislation falls into four areas:
- Minimum legal age to purchase or consume alcohol (legal drinking age, LDA).
- Maximum blood alcohol concentration (BAC) for drivers (and operators of other dangerous machinery).
- Guidelines for sensible drinking.
- Restrictions covering the marketing, packaging and sale of alcohol.

Legal Age to Purchase and Legal Drinking Age (LDA)

In many countries a minimum age is set at which it becomes legal to drink and/or purchase alcohol. They can be different. Together they limit minors' access to alcohol. Most drinking-age legislation does not cover drinking in the home with parental permission and supervision.

Blood Alcohol Concentration (BAC) Limits

A person's BAC level measures the amount of alcohol in the blood by recording the milligrams of ethanol per millilitre of blood. Most countries around the world have legal BAC limits for drivers, ranging from 0.0 mg/mL to 0.8 mg/mL, with different penalties applying for breaking the law.

Sensible Drinking Guidelines

Recommendations on drinking levels considered 'minimum risk' for men and women exist in many countries. Information included in guidelines also defines a standard drink or unit (which differ in each country) and offers advice to those deemed to be at an increased risk of harm.

Official 'drinks' or 'units' generally contain between 8 g and 14 g of pure ethanol, although the measure varies among countries – there is no international consensus on a single standard drink size.

Responsible Marketing of Alcohol

As alcohol is harmful if drunk in excess, many laws, codes and guidelines exist to regulate and ensure that alcohol is produced, marketed and sold in a socially responsible manner. There are voluntary codes and also individual company codes. Many are reinforced with independent complaints panels.

ALCOHOL AND HEALTH

Are There Any Health Benefits to Moderate Drinking?

With moderate drinking, as part of a healthy diet and lifestyle, the risk of developing cardiovascular disease and the risk of death from cardiovascular disease may be reduced, especially for men over 40 and post-menopausal women for whom the risk factors for heart disease and strokes are highest. Statistically there are no health benefits for younger age groups. It is not recommended that anyone should start drinking for health reasons.

When Not to Drink

Even mild intoxication can impair the ability to perform potentially dangerous tasks, such as driving a car, because alcohol slows down your reactions. As no safe threshold of consumption has been established during pregnancy, it is recommended that pregnant women and those planning to conceive should avoid alcohol. Alcohol does not mix with certain medications and your doctor will advise you if this is the case. Those with a history of mental illness or addiction should avoid alcohol.

Alcohol and its Metabolism

Alcohol is absorbed by the body through the stomach and small intestines. Food slows down the rate of absorption – that's why alcohol affects you more quickly on an empty stomach. Alcohol then enters the bloodstream and travels throughout the body within a few minutes.

The body can't store alcohol, so it has to break it down – mostly via the liver. The body's ability to process alcohol depends on age, weight and sex, but on average the body breaks down alcohol at a rate of roughly one standard drink per hour.

Drinking Too Much, Too Fast

Alcohol is a mood-altering substance, and the more you drink the greater the effect. Getting drunk impairs your judgement and can increase risky behaviour, which could result in:
- an increased risk of sustaining injuries and being involved in accidents
- a greater risk of engaging in unsafe sex, which could result in sexually transmitted infections and unplanned pregnancies
- an increased risk of being robbed or going home with a stranger

- an increased risk of fights, arguments and relationship problems
- an increased risk of gaining a criminal record
- in extreme cases, alcoholic poisoning, coma, brain damage and death.

Getting drunk or drinking heavily on a regular basis increases the risks of:
- alcohol dependence or alcoholism
- sexual difficulties, including impotence
- cirrhosis of the liver and alcoholic fatty liver
- cardiac arrest and stroke
- pancreatitis
- stomach disorders, such as ulcers
- certain types of cancer, especially of the aerodigestive tract and breast cancer.

ALCOHOL AND HEALTH MYTHS
If you feel fine you are fine
Just because you don't feel drunk or have any side effects from drinking too much regularly, you may still be storing up problems, both in the short and long term. No matter how 'used' to drinking you are, your liver can only break down approximately 10 g (a small drink) an hour. This means you can be over the drink drive limit many hours after drinking heavily. In the long term, liver disease is essentially 'a silent disease', meaning you don't show any symptoms until damage is advanced.

If I drink lots regularly my body becomes tolerant of alcohol
It is true that you will 'hold your drink better' and feel drunk less easily as you drink more often, but this doesn't mean the harm heavy drinking does to your body reduces. Drinking regularly more than the responsible drinking guidelines is harmful to the body.

Eating food with alcohol minimises the effect on the body
It is always a good idea to eat before or while you are drinking: food helps absorb alcohol and so it enters your bloodstream more slowly. Eventually, however, the same amount of alcohol will be in your system, so while eating delays the effect of alcohol, it does not lessen the quantity to be broken down by your liver and alcohol will stay in your system for longer.

Drinking water before going to bed will dilute the damaging effects
It is a good idea to drink water before going to bed as alcohol is dehydrating, so the water could lessen the 'hangover' effects of drinking heavily. However, the same amount of alcohol will remain in your body for your liver to break down, so the damaging effects of excess are not reduced.

I can drive safely after just a couple of drinks
As we are all different sizes, weights, heights, and with different metabolisms, it is impossible to gauge a safe level to drink before being over the legal BAC limit. Absorption will also depend on whether you have eaten and how well or how tired you are. The best advice is to nominate a designated non-drinking driver, or to plan an alternative way to get home.

After a good night's sleep, I will sleep off the effects of alcohol
Your body (liver) can break down approximately 10 g (a small drink) an hour, and there's nothing you can do to speed that up. Coffee, food or water may make you feel better, but if you've consumed five glasses of wine (20 g a glass) it will take 10 hours for the alcohol to break down, so you risk being over the limit the next morning.

People in their twenties and thirties gain health benefits from moderate levels of red wine consumption, because of the antioxidants it contains
The protective effects of moderate alcohol consumption only apply to post-menopausal women and men over 40, where the risk of heart attack and stroke increase significantly. This is because alcohol thins the blood, helping avoid clots, and stimulates the liver to expel damaging LDL cholesterol. Polyphenols and tannins (antioxidants) may offer extra benefits by relaxing artery walls and protecting against damaging free radicals, but our ability to absorb antioxidants and use them effectively is still uncertain. Alcohol should be drunk for pleasure and relaxation and not for any conceived health benefit.

This text has been supplied by Alcohol in Moderation (AIM). For further details about any of the issues raised here we recommend you consult the Alcohol in Moderation (AIM) websites: www.drinkingandyou.com and www.alcoholinmoderation.com

6

Storage and Service

In order to get the best out of any wine it is important that wines are stored correctly and served at the correct temperature. It may not be necessary to invest in expensive storage units and elaborate devices: simple common sense and standard equipment that is widely available are often enough to ensure that wines are enjoyed at their best.

STORAGE OF WINE

If a wine is incorrectly stored it can affect the flavour and, in severe cases, the wine will become faulty.

The following general points should be followed when storing wine:

- For long-term storage, the temperature for all wines should be cool and constant, preferably between 10°C and 15°C, as extremes of cold and heat can cause damage. One of the worst places for long-term storage is in a kitchen, due to the wide fluctuations in temperature. Extended periods of refrigeration can cause corks to harden and lose their elasticity, with the result that the seal fails and air can attack the wine causing it to become stale. Sparkling wines lose their fizz.
- Store wine that is sealed with a cork on its side to ensure the cork remains in contact with the wine. If the cork dries out it can let in air, and the air will oxidise the wine. Wines that are sealed with a screwcap can be stored standing up without any risk.
- Keep wines away from strong light. Natural sunshine or artificial light will heat the wine and it will become stale and old before its time. Artificial light can cause unpleasant flavours to develop in some wines.
- Keep wine away from vibrations, in order for it to lie undisturbed.

SERVICE OF WINE
Service Temperatures

It is worth considering the following points.

Room temperature is often the recommended temperature for full-bodied red wine. However, with the widespread use of air-conditioning and central heating, rooms can often be either too hot or too cold. If reds are too cold, they will taste thin and harsh. The most gentle

way to warm them is to allow the bottle to warm up slowly or by holding the bowl of the glass in your hands. Do not warm reds on a radiator, as the sudden exposure to extreme heat can irretrievably damage the wine. Red wines that gradually reach temperatures in excess of 18°C will appear to lose their freshness and the flavours will become muddled. Once they are cooled down they regain their balance.

Ice buckets or wine coolers are often used to keep white, rosé and sparkling wines cold. An ice bucket should be filled three-quarters full with equal quantities of ice and water so that the bottle is fully surrounded by iced water. The water is then able to transfer the heat from the bottle to melt the ice. Air acts as an insulator and a bottle in ice alone will chill very slowly until some of the ice has melted.

STYLE OF WINE	EXAMPLE OF STYLE OF WINE	SERVICE TEMPERATURE
Medium/full-bodied, oaked white	White Burgundy, Fumé Blanc	Lightly chilled 10–13°C (50–55°F)
Light/medium-bodied white	Muscadet, Pinot Grigio, New Zealand Sauvignon Blanc, Fino Sherry	Chilled 7–10°C (45–50°F)
Sweet wines	Sauternes, Sweet Muscats	Well chilled 6–8°C (43–45°F)
Sparkling wines	Champagne, Cava, Asti	Well chilled 6–10°C (43–50°F)
Light-bodied red	Beaujolais, Valpolicella	Lightly chilled 13°C (55°F)
Medium/full-bodied red	Red Bordeaux, Red Burgundy, Rioja, Australian Shiraz, Châteauneuf-du-Pape, Barolo, Amarone della Valpolicella, Vintage Port	Room temperature 15–18°C (59–64°F)

Glassware

An enormous range of glass shapes and sizes is used for the service of wine, each designed to emphasise a particular wine's characteristics. The use of the correct glass will enhance the drinking experience.

- **Red wines** are best served in larger-sized glasses. This will allow air to come into contact with a large wine surface and develop the aromas and flavours.
- **White** and **rosé wines** require medium-sized glasses so that the fresh, fruit characteristics are gathered and directed towards the top of the glass.
- **Sparkling wines** are best served in flute glasses. This shape enhances the effect of the bubbles (and thus the wine's aroma), allowing them to travel through a larger volume of the wine before bursting at the top of the glass. For this reason the old-style, saucer-shaped glasses are completely inappropriate, as the bubbles are very quickly lost.
- **Fortified wines** should be served in small glasses to emphasise the fruit characteristics rather than the alcohol. However, the glass should be large enough to allow swirling and nosing.

Clean glassware is of the utmost importance, as even the slightest taint can ruin the flavour of the wine. This can also apply to 'clean' glasses from a dishwasher; it is worth checking the glasses to make sure no detergent or salt residue remains in the glass as this can give strange flavours to wines. In the case of sparkling wine, it will make it lose its sparkle more quickly. The best way to prepare glasses is to polish them before each use. This will make sure the glasses are clean and free of finger marks and dust. The best cloth to use is a linen one, as this will not leave small pieces of fluff in the glass.

Opening a Bottle of Still Wine

- Remove the top of the capsule, by cutting round below the lip of the bottle. This can be done with a capsule remover or knife.
- Wipe the neck of the bottle with a clean cloth.
- Draw the cork as gently and cleanly as possible using your selected corkscrew.
- Give the neck of the bottle a final clean inside and out.
- Pour a sample into a glass to check the wine's condition.

A line-up of glasses for different styles of beverage. From left to right: sparkling wine, Port, white wine, spirits, red wine.

Opening a Bottle of Sparkling Wine

There is considerable pressure in a bottle of sparkling wine. Chilling to the correct temperature helps to reduce this. Even when the wine is chilled, it is possible for the cork to spring violently from the bottle and injure someone.

- Remove the foil and loosen the wire cage.
- The cork must be held securely in place from the moment the wire cage is loosened.
- Tilt the bottle at an angle of about 30°, gripping the cork, and use the other hand to grip the base of the bottle.
- Turn the bottle, not the cork.
- Hold the cork steady, resisting its tendency to fly out, and ease it slowly out of the bottle.
- The gas pressure should be released with a quiet 'phut', not an explosion and a flying cork.

Decanting Wine

Wines with a heavy deposit need to be decanted. This deposit is quite natural and is formed during the ageing process of many good red wines. Some young wines benefit from the aeration that occurs by being decanted, although this can be done easily by swirling the wine in a glass. Note that 'airing' a wine by opening a bottle some time before service does absolutely no good at all. Too little of the wine is in contact with the air for it to have any effect.

- First remove the bottle horizontally from its rack and place in a decanting basket if available. Alternatively, hold carefully, making sure the deposit is not agitated.
- Very gently remove the top of the capsule and clean the shoulder and neck of the bottle. Very gently remove the cork.
- Remove the bottle from the basket, being careful not to disturb the deposit. Holding the bottle in front of a light, pour the wine carefully into the decanter until the deposit can be seen near the neck. At this point stop pouring.

ORDERING WINE

It is useful to know how many measures you can get from a standard 75 cL bottle. This will help you work out how many bottles you would need for an order.

6 x 125 mL glasses   ♈ ♈ ♈ ♈ ♈

4 x 175 mL glasses   ♈ ♈ ♈ ♈

3 x 250 mL glasses   ♈ ♈ ♈

METHODS USED TO PRESERVE WINE

If a wine is not consumed as soon as it is opened it will lose its aromatic intensity in a matter of days and after that it will oxidise and develop vinegar aromas. The simplest way to extend a wine's life is to replace the closure and store the wine in a fridge. This will only extend the life of the wine by a few days. There are other methods that can be used to extend a wine's life for a greater period of time:

- Vacuum systems – These are systems where the oxygen is removed from the bottle and the bottle is sealed. These are unsuitable for sparkling wines (which will lose their bubbles).
- Blanket systems – These systems work on the principle of blanketing the wine with a gas heavier than oxygen to form a protective layer between the wine and air.

Inexpensive devices that work using either of these principles are widely available.

Chardonnay

Chardonnay is not an aromatic grape variety. The delicacy of its fruit makes it suitable for expressing the oak and yeast-derived flavours described below. In certain areas it can produce restrained wines sometimes described as 'steely' or 'minerally'.

7

THE FLAVOURS OF CHARDONNAY

Chardonnay is a white grape variety that is unusual because it can make attractive wines in regions of varying climates, ranging from cool (Chablis) to hot (parts of California). However, its style varies greatly depending on where it is grown. In cool regions such as Chablis, it can offer green fruit (apple, pear) with citrus and occasionally vegetable notes (cucumber). In moderate regions, such as most of Burgundy and some premium New World regions, the wines may taste of white stone fruit (peach) with citrus notes and hints of melon. Hot regions, such as many New World sites, result in the expression of more tropical fruit notes (peach, banana and pineapple, and even mango and fig).

Many of the flavours commonly associated with Chardonnay wines come not from the grape variety, but from winemaking techniques. When they appear, the dairy (butter, cream) flavours are the side-products of a process called **malolactic fermentation**, which is sometimes used to soften harsh acids. The **lees** (dead yeast cells left behind after fermentation has finished) can also be stirred through the wine to add a creamy texture and savoury flavours. Flavours of toast, vanilla and coconut occur because of **oak** treatment.

Not all premium Chardonnays taste of oak. Chardonnay has quite delicate flavours, and the regional characteristics the fruit can display are easily obliterated by excess oak. Wines such as Chablis work well because of their purity of fruit and little or no use of oak. Where the fruit is of sufficient quality, the wine can be fermented and aged in small new oak barrels, and the oak and fruit will balance each other.

Chardonnay wines tend to be quite full-bodied, with a weighty, creamy texture. The best Chardonnays age well, developing a honeyed, nutty, savoury complexity.

PREMIUM CHARDONNAY REGIONS
White Burgundy

The classic region for Chardonnay wines, and arguably where this grape variety finds its best expression (certainly its most expensive), is Burgundy, in eastern France. The word 'Chardonnay' rarely appears on the labels of these wines, and as such they are labelled according to the region, the district, the village or sometimes the vineyard from which the grapes originate. Chardonnay is grown throughout Burgundy. Wines made from grapes grown throughout the region are simply labelled as **Bourgogne**.

Chablis has a cool climate. The bone-dry wines it produces have high acidity and can be quite austere, with green fruit and citrus notes. Many of the wines have a recognisable smoky, flinty, mineral signature. These characteristics are more pronounced in wines labelled *Premier Cru* or *Grand Cru*. With very few exceptions, oak flavours are not detectable in these wines.

The **Côte d'Or** is the heart of Burgundy. It has a moderate climate that provides ideal conditions for high-quality Chardonnay. Chardonnay wines come mainly from the southern half (known as the Côte de Beaune), and are usually sold under the name of the village from which the grapes originate. The most famous of these are **Meursault** and **Puligny-Montrachet**. Complexity and body are often added to these wines by fermenting them in small oak barrels, and ageing them in contact with the yeast left over from fermentation. The resulting wines are full-bodied, and offer a complex succession of different flavours including citrus, white stone and tropical fruit, oak, spice and savoury notes. Chardonnay wines from the Le Montrachet vineyard are judged by many to be the very finest dry white wines in the world. They have prices to match.

CHARDONNAY

0   200   400   600 Km

0   100   200   300 Miles

N

U.K.

BELGIUM   GERMANY

LUX.

50°N   50°N

Paris

CHAMPAGNE
(SPARKLING WINE)

FRANCE

BURGUNDY

CHABLIS

CÔTE DE BEAUNE

MEURSAULT

PULIGNY-MONTRACHET

MÂCONNAIS

POUILLY-FUISSÉ

SWITZ.

46°N   46°N

ATLANTIC
OCEAN

ITALY

PAYS D'OC IGP

42°N   42°N

SPAIN

MEDITERRANEAN
SEA

Ripe Chardonnay grapes in Burgundy. White grapes often take on a golden colour as they ripen.

The **Mâconnais** is the most southerly major region for White Burgundy. It is also a source of large volumes of moderately priced, light, fruity (melon, citrus) Chardonnay wines, most of which see little or no oak and are sold as **Mâcon**. **Pouilly-Fuissé** offers full-bodied Chardonnay wines, often with tropical fruit (pineapple, melon) and oak flavours. These come from a series of steep suntrap slopes at the far south of the Mâconnais.

Australia and New Zealand

In Australia, Chardonnay is planted widely throughout the vineyard regions, and made in a wide range of styles. The main regions for premium Chardonnay include the cooler parts of Victoria (such as the **Yarra Valley**), the **Adelaide Hills** Region in South Australia, and the **Margaret River** Region in Western Australia. The classic Australian Chardonnay style has pronounced fruit (fresh citrus and melon) and well-integrated oak flavours, but examples with a more restrained fruit character and less or no oak are becoming more common.

Production in New Zealand is too small to offer Chardonnay in the very lowest price brackets. Although it does have some large-volume brands, **Marlborough** is an important area for premium Chardonnay, with high natural crisp acidity with pronounced citrus and tropical fruit flavours, and mineral notes. Most of the best wines have pronounced oak flavours.

USA

Chardonnay is grown widely throughout the premium grape-growing regions of California. Most premium Chardonnay comes from regions that are cooled by breezes and morning mists blown in from the Pacific Ocean. This slows the ripening of the grapes, and this long ripening period allows intense, complex flavours to build up. The wines may be labelled simply as **California**, or they may state a more specific location (such as Russian River, **Sonoma** or **Carneros**). Some premium producers even follow the Burgundian model by bottling their wines in small quantities according to the individual vineyard. Californian Chardonnays vary widely

Producer. —————

Region: Sonoma County is a broad area that allows the producer to blend wine from several different vineyard sites.

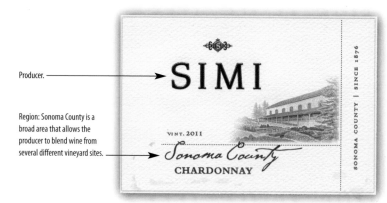

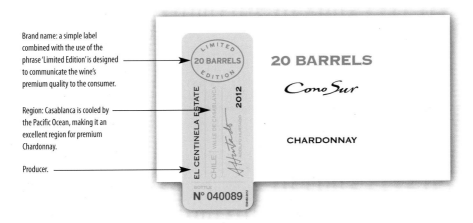

Brand name: a simple label combined with the use of the phrase 'Limited Edition' is designed to communicate the wine's premium quality to the consumer.

Region: Casablanca is cooled by the Pacific Ocean, making it an excellent region for premium Chardonnay.

Producer.

in style. Many are very full-bodied, with intense, rich citrus and ripe peach flavours, and are heavily oaked. Others can be very savoury and reminiscent of those from the Côte d'Or.

South America and South Africa
In **Chile**, although some very high-quality Chardonnays are produced in the Central Valley, the **Casablanca Valley** sub-region north-west of Santiago is establishing itself as an area for premium Chardonnay. Cool sea breezes and morning fogs slow down ripening and allow time for flavours to build up, while acids are retained. Banana and melon flavours are often enhanced by barrel fermentation and oak ageing.

In **Argentina** there are some premium Chardonnay sites within the province of **Mendoza**. Here the high altitude and cool night-time temperatures help produce wines with intense fruit flavours often with a spicy oak character.

South Africa, particularly in the cooler coastal parts such as **Walker Bay**, is a source of some very fine Chardonnays in a variety of styles.

BULK-PRODUCTION REGIONS FOR INEXPENSIVE CHARDONNAY
Chardonnay wines are very popular on international markets. Premium vineyard sites for Chardonnay are limited in area. Fortunately for Chardonnay-lovers, this is a grape variety that can tolerate a wide range of soils and climates, and can still show some of its soft texture and buttery-melon fruit flavours even at high yields. In order to hit low price points and still make a profit, producers need to make large volumes and take advantage of economies of scale in production, distribution and marketing. In order to obtain large volumes, wines from a number of sites may be blended together. The wine will be sold simply as coming from **South Eastern Australia**, **Western Cape**, **California**, **Central Valley (Chile)**, **Pays d'Oc IGP** or Vin de France. Chardonnay wines are also found at inexpensive prices in **Southern Italy** and **Argentina**.

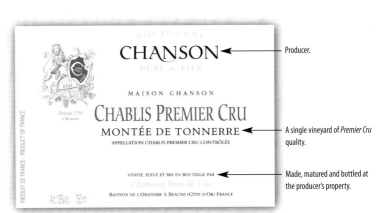

Producer.

A single vineyard of *Premier Cru* quality.

Made, matured and bottled at the producer's property.

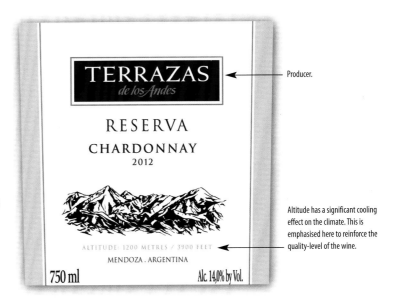

Producer.

Altitude has a significant cooling effect on the climate. This is emphasised here to reinforce the quality-level of the wine.

Generally, large-volume Chardonnays will be fermented, blended and stored in stainless steel vats until they are ready for packaging and sale. Oak flavours are often added in the form of staves or chips, although occasionally a proportion of the wine may be fermented or aged in oak barrels.

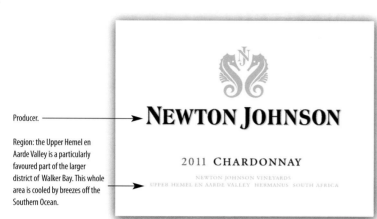

Producer.

Region: the Upper Hemel en Aarde Valley is a particularly favoured part of the larger district of Walker Bay. This whole area is cooled by breezes off the Southern Ocean.

CHARDONNAY IN BLENDS

Chardonnay produces its finest still wines unblended. For the low-price, high-volume market, other grape varieties that are more widely available at a lower price may be used to stretch the Chardonnay component. The classic example of this is Semillon-Chardonnay (or Chardonnay-Semillon, depending on which variety dominates) from Australia, although volumes of this are now falling. In South Africa and California, Colombard-Chardonnay and Chardonnay-Chenin Blanc blends work in much the same way.

Similarly, in European regions, unfashionable local grape varieties may be blended with Chardonnay to make a marketable wine, providing a viable outlet for grapes that may otherwise struggle to find a buyer.

One other grape variety that does seem to provide a successful pairing is Viognier. Its oily texture and full body merge well with Chardonnay, and the aromatic Viognier gives a little extra peachy, floral character to the wine.

Pinot Noir

Pinot Noir is very fussy about where it is grown, which makes it a very difficult variety for grape growers. However, it is a very easy variety to drink. Unlike some other black grape varieties, such as Cabernet Sauvignon, many Pinot Noir wines have soft, light tannins and do not need time in the bottle to evolve attractive flavours. Instead, they are enjoyable to drink at all stages of their life.

8

THE FLAVOURS OF PINOT NOIR

Pinot Noir is a black grape variety with thin skins, and the resulting wines are usually light in colour with low to medium levels of tannin. It likes moderate or cool climates, although in regions that are too cool, the grapes will not ripen and the wines will have excessive vegetal flavours (cabbage, wet leaves). In a few regions, the right balance is found, and the resulting wines display red fruit (strawberry, raspberry, cherry), and develop vegetal and animal nuances (wet leaves, mushroom, gamey-meaty aromas) with age. In hot regions, it loses its delicate flavours, and the wines are excessively jammy.

Some Pinot Noirs are able to develop great complexity with age. However, except for the very best wines from Burgundy and some other premium sites, most Pinot Noirs are best consumed while they are youthful and fruity.

It is common to mature the best Pinot Noirs in oak, but the toast and vanilla notes of new oak can easily overpower this variety's delicate flavours.

Pinot Noir grapes ripening in Burgundy.

PREMIUM PINOT NOIR REGIONS

Red Burgundy

The classic region for Pinot Noir wines is in Burgundy (Bourgogne). This is where Pinot Noir's fussiness is most fully exploited: wines from the different villages show slightly different aspects of this variety, so they are given their own appellations.

A **Bourgogne AC** should be a medium-bodied red with a balance of red-fruit and savoury aromas, light tannins and medium to high acidity. Wines from the individual villages, such as **Gevrey-Chambertin**, **Nuits-Saint-Georges**, **Beaune** and **Pommard**, generally offer more intensity, complexity and length, particularly those from *Premier Cru* vineyard sites within the villages. *Grand Cru* Red Burgundies, such as Le Chambertin, are the most powerful, long-lived and complex Pinot Noir wines in the world, selling at very high prices because of their quality and rarity.

Germany

Germany produces large volumes of Pinot Noir (Spätburgunder in German), mainly in the southern regions of the **Pfalz** and **Baden**. These have a cool climate and the typical style is light-bodied with pronounced, perfumed red berry fruit and light tannins. Fuller-bodied, barrel-aged styles are also made.

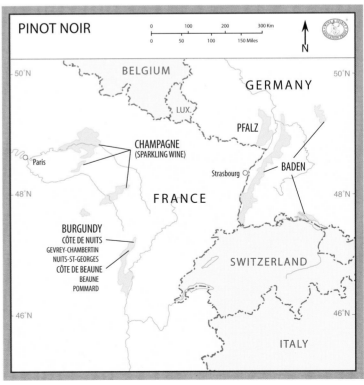

PINOT NOIR

| 0 | 100 | 200 | 300 Km |
| 0 | 50 | 100 | 150 Miles |

BELGIUM
GERMANY
LUX.
PFALZ
CHAMPAGNE (SPARKLING WINE)
Paris
BADEN
Strasbourg
FRANCE
BURGUNDY
CÔTE DE NUITS
GEVREY-CHAMBERTIN
NUITS-ST-GEORGES
CÔTE DE BEAUNE
BEAUNE
POMMARD
SWITZERLAND
ITALY

LABELLING IN BURGUNDY

In Burgundy the appellations form a clear quality hierarchy. At the bottom are the regional appellations such as **Bourgogne AC**, which account for half of the region's production. Next in the hierarchy are the commune or village appellations such as **Beaune**, **Gevrey-Chambertin** and **Nuits-Saint-Georges**. At the top of the hierarchy are single vineyards' appellations. Vineyards are specific plots of land and rarely, if ever, change in size. Each commune with *Premier Cru* vineyards has a separate AC for these, and each individual *Grand Cru* vineyard has its own AC. Not all producers will choose to make the whole range. However, one such producer who does is Louis Jadot. Here are some examples to reflect this hierarchy:

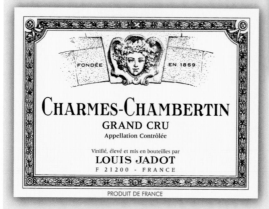

In Burgundy, and elsewhere in France, the word **domaine** can appear on a label. This refers to a producer who makes wine exclusively from grapes grown in their own vineyards. The choice of making *domaine* or non-domaine wines is down to the decision of the producer. For example, only some of the Louis Jadot labels (seen above) have this term stated on the label, and therefore only these are *domaine* wines, even though all of the wines are made by the same producer. For these wines, Jadot would have bought in grapes, juice or finished wines to be sold under their name. These are négociant/merchant wines – terms rarely seen on the label.

Australia and New Zealand

New Zealand Pinot Noirs are generally more full-bodied, with lower acidity and more intense fruit than the wines from Burgundy. Spicy notes often accompany the red fruit flavours (cherry, strawberry). **Central Otago** makes the ripest, most intense New Zealand Pinot Noirs. The variety is also grown in **Marlborough**, where a lighter style is made, and much of the fruit is used for sparkling wine.

Most Australian regions are too hot for Pinot Noir, although some premium-quality wines are being made in sites that benefit from the cooling effects of ocean breezes or altitude, such as the **Yarra Valley** and **Mornington Peninsula** regions in Victoria. Here the style of Pinot Noir can vary from light and delicate with fragrant aromas, to those with richer fruit flavours (strawberry, plum, dark cherry) and more structured, riper tannins.

USA

Most of the regions in **California** are too warm for good-quality Pinot Noir, but good examples can be found in **Carneros** and in cooler parts of **Sonoma** and **Santa Barbara** Counties. Californian Pinot Noirs tend to be full-bodied. Most are intensely fruity, with red fruit flavours (red cherry, strawberry), but some display pronounced animal and vegetal characteristics (leather, meat, wet leaves). A suitably moderate climate is found further north in **Oregon**, where some very high-quality Pinot Noir wines are produced.

South America and South Africa

The **Casablanca** and San Antonio valleys in Chile are emerging as sources of intensely fruity Pinot Noirs, often with flavours of strawberry jam.

South Africa also makes some high-quality Pinot Noirs, in small quantities, from coastal sites such as **Walker Bay**.

BULK-PRODUCTION REGIONS FOR INEXPENSIVE PINOT NOIR

Because Pinot Noir is such a tricky grape to grow, there are few inexpensive sources. Many of the regions that produce large volumes of inexpensive varietal wines,

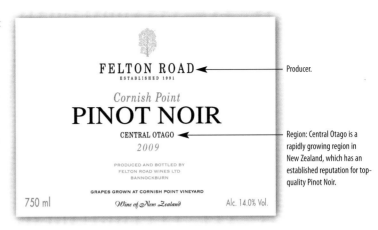

Producer.

Region: Central Otago is a rapidly growing region in New Zealand, which has an established reputation for top-quality Pinot Noir.

such as California (Central Valley), Australia (Murray-Darling) and most of France's Pays d'Oc IGP, are simply too hot for Pinot Noir. **Chile** successfully produces some inexpensive Pinot Noir wines in a soft, fruity style.

PINOT NOIR IN BLENDS

Pinot Noir produces its finest still wines unblended (although it is used as a component of many sparkling wines, including most Champagne). In Burgundy, Pinot Noir can be blended with Gamay but, apart from a few obscure exceptions, a red Burgundy will be 100 per cent Pinot Noir.

9 Cabernet Sauvignon and Merlot

These two grape varieties are often grown together and blended together. Merlot is added to Cabernet Sauvignon to produce a wine that is more easily drinkable, as the Merlot supplies softness and body to an otherwise quite austere wine. Cabernet Sauvignon is often added to Merlot to give tannin, acidity and aromatic fruit. The classic region for such blends is Bordeaux, but it is common for a small amount of blending to occur in New World varietally labelled wines, even though this is not mentioned on the label.

THE FLAVOURS OF CABERNET SAUVIGNON

Cabernet Sauvignon is a black grape variety that gives deeply coloured wines that have lots of tannin and acidity, and strong aromas. Typical flavours include black fruits (blackcurrant, black cherry), often accompanied by herbaceous notes (bell pepper, mint). Oak is frequently used to age the premium wines, softening the tannins and adding oaky flavours (smoke, vanilla, coffee, cedar). Cabernet Sauvignon needs a moderate or hot climate; it cannot ripen in cool climates or cool years. Wines made from under-ripe Cabernet Sauvignon can be very harsh and astringent with unpleasant herbaceous flavours. Wines from hot climates are fuller-bodied, with softer tannins, more black cherry fruit and a less herbaceous character.

Because of the intense fruit flavours, and high levels of tannin and acidity, Cabernet Sauvignon is a good variety for making wines that age well.

THE FLAVOURS OF MERLOT

Merlot is also a black grape variety. It gives wines that are less aromatic, with less intense flavours and lighter tannins and acidity than Cabernet Sauvignon, but generally with more body and higher alcohol. Flavours typically fall into one of two groups, depending on how ripe the grapes are. The common international style, made from grapes grown in hot climates or over-ripe grapes grown in moderate climates, shows a black fruit character (blackberry, black plum, black cherry), full body, medium or low acidity, high alcohol and medium levels of gentle tannins. Some super-ripe versions display fruitcake and chocolate flavours. Less common is a more elegant style, possible in moderate or cooler climates, showing a red fruit character (strawberry, red berry, plum), some herbal notes (mint), and a little more tannin and acidity. Like Cabernet Sauvignon, the best Merlot wines are often aged in oak, gaining spicy and oaky flavours (vanilla, coffee).

PREMIUM CABERNET SAUVIGNON AND MERLOT REGIONS
Bordeaux

Bordeaux is the classic home for these grape varieties. It has a moderate, maritime climate with long, warm autumns that provide ideal conditions for Cabernet Sauvignon and Merlot. The region is based around the Gironde estuary in southwest France, where the Garonne and Dordogne rivers meet. For premium-quality wines, it is helpful to focus on two zones within the Bordeaux region.

West and south of the Gironde and Garonne lies the zone many refer to as the Left Bank. Running from north to south, the main appellations here are the **Médoc**, **Haut-Médoc** (including the communes **Pauillac** and **Margaux**), and **Graves** (including the commune **Pessac-Léognan**). Here, Cabernet Sauvignon is the dominant variety. The best sites are on gravel mounds that drain water away and retain heat to aid ripening. The wines are medium or full-bodied, with high levels of tannin and acidity, medium alcohol, and long length. They can be very tough when young, but with age the tannins soften, and the flavours of black fruit (blackcurrant, black cherry) and toasty fragrant oak develop into vegetal, tobacco and cedar complexity. The very best wines come from

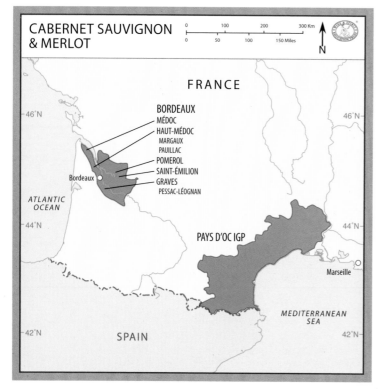

Premium Cabernet Sauvignon vineyard in Bordeaux. The gravelly soil helps store heat to aid ripening, and rapidly drains away excess water.

the *Cru Classé* châteaux. These are among the world's most complex long-lived red wines.

The other major production zone for premium-quality wines, the Right Bank, lies north and east of the Gironde and Dordogne. The most important appellations are **Saint-Émilion AC** (the best wines from here are labelled as **Saint-Émilion *Grand Cru* AC**) and **Pomerol AC**. Merlot is the dominant variety here, and the wines are generally softer in style than those from the Left Bank. They typically have medium tannin levels, medium acidity, and a red fruit character (plum, red berry), developing cedar and tobacco notes as they age.

Many premium-quality Bordeaux wines are made outside of the most prestigious appellations. These are labelled simply as **Bordeaux AC** or **Bordeaux Supérieur AC** (a designation that requires a higher level of alcohol than basic Bordeaux AC). These medium-bodied dry reds generally have medium tannin levels and acidity, and a mixture of red and black fruit flavours from the Merlot and Cabernet Sauvignon components. They are generally best consumed while quite young, but some can benefit from bottle age.

Australia and New Zealand

Cabernet Sauvignon is widely grown in Australia, and two regions have established themselves as modern classics. **Coonawarra** Cabernet often displays intense, structured wines with distinctive cassis, mint and eucalyptus flavours, accompanying the black fruit (black cherry) and oak notes (toast, vanilla). **Margaret River** in Western Australia produces varietal Cabernet Sauvignon and Cabernet-Merlot blends. These generally have high tannin levels, with black fruit and herb flavours (blackcurrant, blackcurrant leaf).

High-quality Cabernet Sauvignons, Merlots and Cabernet-Merlot blends are made in the **Hawke's Bay** area of New Zealand's North Island. These typically have medium or high acidity and tannins, and herb aromas (cedar, blackcurrant leaf).

USA

In **California**, Cabernet Sauvignon is the most widely planted black grape. The **Napa Valley** provides ideal conditions for Cabernet Sauvignon and is also a source of some very good Merlots. **Rutherford** and **Oakville** are specifically known for premium Cabernet Sauvignons. These wines typically have high levels of soft, ripe tannin, and are deeply coloured with black cherry and oak flavours. In Sonoma, **Alexander Valley** has a reputation for soft-textured, full-bodied Cabernet Sauvignons. Premium Californian Merlots are generally full-bodied, with flavours of soft black fruit, fruitcake and oak. The extremely dry, sunny climate of Columbia Valley in eastern Washington State also provides excellent conditions for the production of deeply coloured, full-bodied Cabernet Sauvignons and Merlots. In both California and

LABELLING IN BORDEAUX

In Bordeaux many of the labelling terms that are used to indicate quality are not linked to the appellation system, nor do they form a neat hierarchy like that used in Burgundy (see Chapter 8).

Across Bordeaux many of the very best wines are permitted to put *Grand Cru Classé* on the label. In Saint-Émilion the classification of *Grand Cru* is linked to the appellation. However, in the Left Bank this is a labelling system, used by many of the best wines, that is independent of the appellation system. Consequently, not all the wines produced in the smallest appellations such as Pauillac and Margaux are considered equal. Châteaux whose wines that are not classified as *Grand Cru Classé* can apply to have them classified with the less prestigious title of *Cru Bourgeois*. Each wine has to apply for *Cru Bourgeois* status annually. This leaves the most basic and inexpensive of the Bordeaux wines simply labelled as **Bordeaux AC** or **Bordeaux Supérieur AC**.

The term **Grand Vin** is often used to indicate the main wine made by the château, no matter how 'grand' or 'humble' the wine or the château. The labels above that highlight the use of this term are Lynch-Bages and Le Grand Chai.

Another labelling term used by many premium-quality Bordeaux wines is the **château**. This term is clearly recognisable on most of the labels shown above. Names of merchant houses are sometimes used, but this is mainly for large-volume inexpensive wines. A château name does not necessarily refer to a grand building. It indicates that the wine has been made from grapes grown on a producer's own land, rather than being made from bought-in wines, grapes or juice. Over time, châteaux can sell or buy land, so the exact plots associated with the château name can change.

Washington, these two varieties sometimes appear blended together, following the Bordeaux model.

South America and South Africa
Chile produces premium-quality varietal and blended wines from Cabernet Sauvignon and Merlot. These often have pronounced herbal characteristics (green bell pepper, blackcurrant leaf) accompanying intense black fruit flavours (black cherry, blackberry). The best regions are the **Maipo Valley**, close to Santiago, and **Colchagua** and **Cachapoal** (parts of the Rapel Valley), further south. Due to previous confusion in the vineyards, some of the wine that is labelled as Merlot is in fact Carmenère (an old, high-quality variety, also originally from Bordeaux and covered in more detail in Chapter 14). This can add intense colour and spiced black fruit flavours (blackberry, liquorice, pepper).

In **Argentina**, Cabernet Sauvignon appears as varietal wines and is blended with Malbec. Traditionally these wines were aged in oak for a long time before release, giving meaty, leathery flavours. Modern styles are much fruitier. Within the hot **Mendoza** region, where most of Argentina's exported wines are made, there are premium sites where climate is moderated by altitude. These sites are the source of fruit for most of Argentina's best red wines.

South Africa produces some very good Cabernet-Merlot blends, as well as pure varietal wines. These typically have less intense fruit and more herb flavours compared with similar wines from Australia or California. Many of the wines from **Stellenbosch** are close to the Bordeaux style, with high levels of tannin and acidity.

BULK-PRODUCTION REGIONS FOR INEXPENSIVE CABERNET SAUVIGNON AND MERLOT
Cabernet Sauvignon is a grape variety that can be cropped at quite high levels, in a range of climates (provided they are not too cool), and still retain some of its black fruit and high tannin character. **Chile** (Central Valley) and **Southern France** (Pays d'Oc IGP) produce large volumes of inexpensive, varietally expressive Cabernet Sauvignons, Merlots and Cabernet-Merlot

Producer.

Region: Napa Valley has a long-established reputation for making some of the world's best and most expensive Cabernet Sauvignons.

blends. **South Africa** (Western Cape), **South Eastern Australia**, **California** and **Argentina** (Mendoza) are also important areas, although they have more success with Cabernet Sauvignon than with Merlot.

Many inexpensive Merlots are rather bland, though inoffensive, which could be why they are so popular. **Northern Italy** produces large volumes of inexpensive, light-bodied Merlot.

Much basic Bordeaux arguably comes under this heading. The best ones are soft, light- or medium-bodied, and Merlot-based.

CABERNET SAUVIGNON AND MERLOT IN BLENDS
Cabernet Sauvignon-Merlot blends have already been described above. In Australia, Shiraz is often used with Cabernet Sauvignon to give the softness and richness that Merlot supplies in Bordeaux and elsewhere. Merlot is sometimes blended with Malbec in Argentina, and both Cabernet Sauvignon and Merlot are blended with Carmenère in Chile. Cabernet Sauvignon is used in many regions to improve wines by adding a little aromatic fruit, colour and tannin.

10   Sauvignon Blanc

Some attribute the success of Sauvignon Blanc to its ability to create clear expectations (clean, crisp, refreshing, unoaked), and meet them. This is in contrast to Chardonnay, which is made in a very wide range of styles, and Riesling, which has failed to communicate its qualities to most wine consumers. We shall see, however, that Sauvignon is capable of more than one style.

THE FLAVOURS OF SAUVIGNON BLANC

Sauvignon Blanc is an aromatic white grape variety. Its wines usually display strong aromas of green fruit and vegetables (gooseberry, elderflower, green bell pepper, asparagus). They are usually high in acidity, medium-bodied, and almost always dry. In order to show its herbaceous-aromatic character, Sauvignon Blanc needs a cool climate, although it will tolerate a moderate one. Wines from moderate regions, however, tend to lack the intense pungent aromatic complexity of wines from premium, cool-climate sites.

Most varietal Sauvignons have no oak flavours, because the style sought is one dominated by refreshing fruitiness. Those that are aged in oak generally come from moderate regions, and the oak can add flavours of toast and spice (vanilla, liquorice). Most varietal Sauvignons do not benefit from bottle age: although they may last, they lose their attractive freshness and rapidly become stale. Sauvignon Blanc, with its high levels of acidity, is also suitable for sweet wines, particularly in Sauternes (see Chapter 16).

PREMIUM SAUVIGNON BLANC REGIONS

Loire Central Vineyards

The villages of **Sancerre** and **Pouilly-Fumé** face each other across the Loire. The cool climate results in dry white wines with high acidity, medium body, with moderate or pronounced aromas. These wines have green fruit and herbaceous aromas (gooseberry, grass, blackcurrant leaf, nettle) and often display a steely character that is similar to Chablis.

Bordeaux

Most premium white Bordeaux is a blend of Sémillon and Sauvignon Blanc, often with the Sémillon dominating. Sauvignon alone is usually a fruity wine with distinctively herbaceous, grassy and elderflower aromas, and is unsuited to ageing. Adding a proportion of Sémillon can help sustain the fruit character, and allows complexity to develop in the bottle. Sémillon wines generally add body to the blend too. Sémillon alone can be rather bland and neutral in youth, and adding a proportion of Sauvignon brings aromatic fruit character and refreshing acidity to the blend. These are dry wines, with medium or high acidity, medium or full-bodied, sometimes with oaky flavours. The very best wines, such as those from *Cru Classé* châteaux in the Pessac-Léognan AC and the best white Graves AC, age well and develop honeyed, toasty complex flavours in the bottle.

Australia and New Zealand

Cool-climate **Marlborough** in South Island, New Zealand, has established itself as a new classic region for very expressive Sauvignon Blanc wines. There is an increasing range of styles as producers experiment and attempt to find a point of difference for their own wines, so some are more restrained, or show hints of oak or lees flavours, or are full-bodied. However, the classic style is dry, with high acidity, no oak, medium-bodied and characterised by intense, pungent, clean, varietal flavours (passion fruit, gooseberry, green pepper, blackcurrant leaf). These wines are best consumed while youthful and fresh, although some enjoy the vegetable (asparagus, pea) notes that develop in the bottle. Sauvignons from New Zealand are typically more aromatically pronounced compared with those from the Loire Valley.

In Australia, the best Sauvignon Blancs come from the Adelaide Hills region. These are intensely fruity and clean in style.

USA

In most parts of **California**, the conditions are too warm for the herbaceous characteristics of Sauvignon Blanc to be retained. Despite the climate, some interesting wines are made, especially in the **Napa Valley**, often labelled as **Fumé Blanc**. Depending on the producer, and the consumer the wine is made for, the style may be unoaked, lightly oaked or even heavily oaked. Compared with the oak-aged Chardonnays from the same region, the oaked Fumé Blancs are generally a little less full-bodied, and higher in acidity. Some of the herbaceous varietal character of the Sauvignon Blanc (grass, asparagus) usually shines through the spicy, oaky flavours (toast, liquorice, vanilla).

South America and South Africa

Chile is emerging as a source of herbaceous, fruit-led premium Sauvignon Blanc, particularly from cooler regions such as **Casablanca** and San Antonio. These wines tend to be highly aromatic and refreshingly fruity, with aromas of citrus, green apple and grassy notes.

South Africa produces high-quality Sauvignon Blancs in broadly two styles. Some are pungent and fruit driven, like those from New Zealand, but usually lighter in body, less intense and complex. Others use oak to make a wine that is less pungent, but can age in the bottle, gaining toasty complexity. These follow the Bordeaux model, but have a more intense, herbaceous character. Both **Constantia** and **Elgin** have a particular reputation for Sauvignon Blanc due to cooling influences. Where Constantia receives a constant cooling air from the sea, Elgin's altitude produces a similar cooling effect, causing the late-ripening of the grapes, and producing intense, fresh Sauvignon Blancs.

BULK-PRODUCTION REGIONS FOR INEXPENSIVE SAUVIGNON BLANC

Outside of the premium Loire appellations, France produces large volumes of inexpensive Sauvignon Blanc.

Region: this allows you to work out the grape variety that has been used. Pouilly-Fumé must be made using 100 per cent Sauvignon Blanc.

Region: Marlborough is the largest and best-known region for Sauvignon Blanc in New Zealand.

The image of the mountains takes its cues from the dramatic landscape of Marlborough, which can be seen in the photograph below.

Machine harvesting of Sauvignon Blanc grapes in Marlborough, New Zealand. This is an efficient method of harvesting grapes, allowing large areas of vineyard to be harvested quickly, when the grapes reach optimal ripeness.

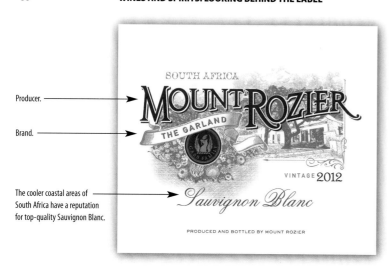

Producer.

Brand.

The cooler coastal areas of South Africa have a reputation for top-quality Sauvignon Blanc.

Some of this is AC wine (e.g. Touraine AC). Much basic white Bordeaux AC (mainly Sauvignon-Sémillon blends) is inexpensive, high-volume wine. Bordeaux is increasingly selling varietally labelled pure Sauvignon Blancs, often at low prices. The Val de Loire and Pays d'Oc IGPs are also important sources of Sauvignon Blanc.

Chile, California and South Africa all produce inexpensive varietal Sauvignons.

SAUVIGNON BLANC IN BLENDS

The most important wines blended with Sauvignon are dry white Bordeaux (see above) and Sauternes (see Chapter 16). Sauvignon Blanc-Semillon blends are also made in Australia, the USA and Chile, but demand for these is decreasing and fewer are being seen on the market.

Syrah and Grenache

The only country outside France to have established a sustained international reputation for premium-quality Syrah (Shiraz) is Australia. Although Grenache is the third most widely planted black grape variety in terms of worldwide vineyard area, most of the vines are found in Spain and southern France. It is most commonly used as part of a blend with other varieties.

11

THE FLAVOURS OF SYRAH/SHIRAZ

This black grape variety is known as Syrah in France and Shiraz in Australia. For simplicity, we will refer to it simply as Syrah.

Syrah grapes, like Cabernet Sauvignon, are small with thick, darkly coloured skins. The wines it makes are deeply coloured, with medium or high levels of tannins and medium acidity. The wines are usually full-bodied and generally have a black fruit (blackberry) and dark chocolate character. In wines from moderate regions, this may be accompanied by hints of herbaceousness, smoked meat and spice (black pepper). In hot regions there are more sweet spice notes (liquorice). With age, the best wines develop animal and vegetal complexities (leather, wet leaves, earth). Syrah does not ripen in cool climates.

Many Syrah wines undergo some oak treatment, either through barrel ageing or the use of chips or staves. These can give toast, smoke, vanilla and coconut flavours to the wine.

THE FLAVOURS OF GRENACHE/GARNACHA

This black grape variety is known as Garnacha in Spain, but in most other regions it is known as Grenache.

Grenache grapes are large, with thin skins, high sugar levels and low acidity. The resulting wines are seldom deep in colour, but are usually very full-bodied. They typically have a red-fruit character (strawberry, raspberry), with spicy notes (white pepper, liquorice). With age, the spicy notes evolve into toffee and leather. Grenache needs a hot climate to ripen.

With their thin skins, it is easy to make rosé wines from Grenache grapes. These tend to be full-bodied and dry, with red fruit flavours (strawberry). Some are light-bodied and fruity, with medium sweetness.

Grenache is used widely for rosé wines in the southern Rhône, southern France and Spain. Most are best consumed while young and vibrant. Very few benefit from ageing, although some are aged in oak, which can give the wines an orange hue and dulls the fruit, but adds savoury complexity.

SYRAH AND GRENACHE TOGETHER

This combination works in a similar way to Cabernet Sauvignon and Merlot, although it is easier to make a complete, satisfying wine from Syrah than 100 per cent

Cabernet. Adding Grenache to Syrah can result in a wine with more alcohol, lower levels of tannin and acidity, and red fruit and extra spice flavours. Adding Syrah to a Grenache-based wine boosts the levels of colour, tannin and acidity, and adds a dark fruit character. Many southern Rhône wines include several other varieties, as well as Syrah and Grenache. Some of these (Mourvèdre and Cinsault) contribute to the character of the wine; others are used because they give high yields and are cheap or easy to grow.

In Australia, a Shiraz-Grenache blend is frequently a full-bodied, fruity red with very soft tannins, a wine that is ideal for serving lightly chilled. There are also some more serious wines made from this combination, particularly from South Australia, which are full-bodied, intense and complex. These serious wines may include other varieties in the blend, such as Mataro (Mourvèdre). Such blends are known colloquially as 'GSMs'.

PREMIUM SYRAH AND GRENACHE REGIONS
The Northern Rhône

This is the classic region for Syrah wines. The finest wines are made from grapes grown on the steep terraces that tower above the Rhône. Many of these terraces are so narrow that no machinery can be used. The vineyard work has to be done by hand, which makes these wines expensive to produce. However, the sunlight and good drainage provide ideal conditions for the production of powerful, complex, ageworthy wines. The best appellations are **Côte Rôtie** and **Hermitage**, although these wines are rare and expensive. **Crozes-Hermitage** is a larger appellation that includes some flatter sites. Its wines are generally less intense and less complex than those of Côte Rôtie and Hermitage, but prices are lower. The wines often display black pepper flavours, tannins and acidity found in Syrah wines from a moderate climate.

The Southern Rhône

Here the valley broadens out and there are no steep slopes. The vineyards stretch far away from the Rhône, covering wide, stony plains. It is hotter and drier here than in the northern Rhône, and the conditions are ideal for Grenache. This is usually blended with other varieties such as Syrah, Mourvèdre and Cinsault.

The main regional appellation is **Côtes du Rhône**. Within this, the better vineyard sites are entitled to label their wines **Côtes du Rhône Villages**. The possibilities available in terms of yields, choice of grape varieties in the blend, and winemaking techniques, means that styles and quality vary considerably. The very cheapest wines tend to be medium-bodied, with light tannins and a simple juicy red fruit and peppery-spice character. The best could pass for Châteauneuf-du-Pape in terms of body, complexity, intensity and length.

There are a number of smaller, highly regarded

LABELLING IN THE RHONE VALLEY

Although the Rhône Valley is considered as one vineyard area, it is naturally divided into two distinct parts: the Northern Rhône and the Southern Rhône. However, even with this division, there is a distinct hierarchy within the wines of the Rhône. The south is home to the generic-level appellation of **Côtes du Rhône AC**. Although this can theoretically be produced in the north, it is rarely seen. Above this is **Côtes du Rhône Villages AC**: a superior sub-region of Côtes du Rhône from a select number of villages, all of which are located in the south.

Of these villages, only a handful are permitted to add their village name to the appellation (e.g. Côtes du Rhône Villages Cairanne). At the top of the appellation system are the *crus*. These are individual areas located in both the north (such as **Crozes-Hermitage**, **Hermitage**, **Côte Rôtie**) and the south (such as **Châteauneuf-du-Pape**), that have been given their own individual AC status.

The labels below have been chosen to reflect this appellation hierarchy found within the Rhône Valley.

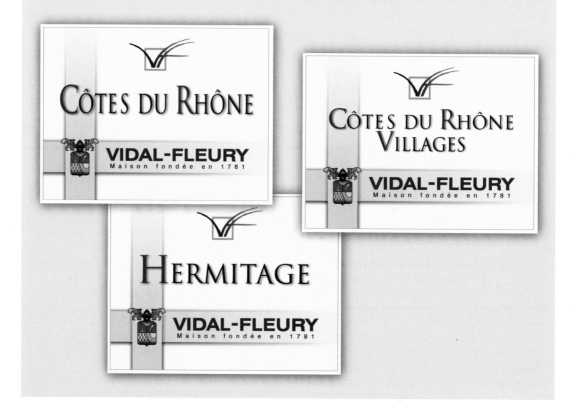

Steep south-facing vineyards on the hill of Hermitage.

appellations in the southern Rhône, of which the most famous is **Châteauneuf-du-Pape**. Some wines are 100 per cent Grenache but most add some Syrah, Mourvèdre and Cinsault. Very few use all of the 13 permitted varieties. Typical Châteauneuf-du-Pape is full-bodied, with medium tannins and low acidity and an intense, complex character that includes red fruit (strawberry), spice (pepper, liquorice) and animal (leather) notes.

South of France
Increasing numbers of premium Grenache and Syrah-based wines are being made in the South of France, from appellations such as **Minervois**. The main varieties in the blend are often Grenache and Carignan (the latter can give tough wines with high levels of acid and tannin). Syrah, as well as Mourvèdre, are used to add complexity to the best wines.

Spain
Garnacha (Grenache) is the most widely planted variety in Spain. It reaches its highest expression in the deep-coloured, powerful, full-bodied wines of **Priorat**, where it is usually the main component of a blend. As such, Priorat has established itself as a premium-quality region for Grenache-based blends. The best of these are very high-quality, complex wines that sell at high prices.

Garnacha can be used as part of the blend (with Tempranillo and other varieties) in **Rioja**, although it is rarely seen in the best wines from this region. It is also used alone or as the main component for rosé wines. The best examples of these come from **Navarra** and Rioja.

Australia
Australia is famed for its Shiraz (Syrah). Shiraz is grown throughout Australia, and is made in different styles.

Perhaps the better known style is for wines that are made from grapes grown in hot climates in regions such as **Hunter Valley**, **McLaren Vale** and the **Barossa Valley**. These wines have flavours that include intense black fruit (blackberry, plum), sweet spices and notes of dark chocolate. Use of oak in these wines can be pronounced, giving flavours of smoke, vanilla and coconut. Shiraz from the Barossa is particularly powerful and is most closely associated with this style. The hot, dry conditions in Barossa and McLaren Vale are also ideal for Grenache, though this is less commonly seen.

Where more moderate conditions are found, in areas such as certain parts of Victoria (Grampians and

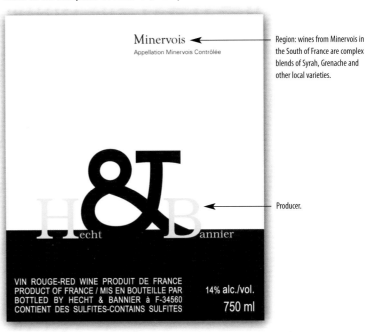

Region: wines from Minervois in the South of France are complex blends of Syrah, Grenache and other local varieties.

Producer.

Producer.

A statement to indicate quality within the producer's range. This has no legal definition.

Region: Barossa is perhaps the classic region for hot climate Shiraz.

wines sometimes mention the origin of each wine used in the blend in the information on the back label, but the geographical indication (GI) will be South Australia.

Other Locations
Shiraz plantings are increasing in countries around the world, including South Africa, where deep-coloured, full-bodied wines are made with aromas of dried fruit (raisin, prune, fruitcake), smoked meat and oak. Full-bodied, dark-fruited Shiraz wines are also made in California and Washington State. New Zealand (Hawke's Bay) and Chile (San Antonio) are showing great promise for more elegant, fruity styles with some peppery spice.

BULK-PRODUCTION REGIONS FOR INEXPENSIVE SYRAH AND GRENACHE
Much wine under the Côtes du Rhône appellation is made in large volumes to be sold at low prices. Similarly, inexpensive blends that include local varieties, as well as Grenache and Syrah, are made in the South of France. They are sold as **Pays d'Oc IGP** and **Languedoc AC**. Large quantities of inexpensive Grenache-led wines are also made in **Spain**.

For inexpensive Shiraz, the main production areas are Riverland, Murray-Darling and Riverina in Australia. (These names do not appear on labels. Instead, the wine will be labelled as **South Eastern Australia**.)

SYRAH AND GRENACHE IN BLENDS
An increasingly fashionable combination is **Shiraz-Viognier**. This follows a northern Rhône tradition of adding some white grapes to the fermentation of Syrah. Viognier helps give the wine a smooth texture, and adds a trace of exotic fruit character.

Syrah blended with Cabernet Sauvignon is described in Chapter 9. Grenache blended with Syrah, Mourvèdre and Cinsault is covered in this chapter. Grenache blended with Tempranillo is covered in Chapter 14.

Heathcote), a different style of Shiraz is made. These wines are more peppery and can be less full-bodied than those from the hotter regions. The best examples are intensely flavoured and complex, and can be quite similar in style to the wines of the Rhône.

Within South Australia, some of the very best Shiraz are multi-regional blends. Blending allows Shiraz wines with different characteristics to contribute to a more complex whole. It also helps producers to make premium wines of consistent quality and style in larger quantities. These

Riesling

Riesling has a pronounced fruity, varietal character which is expressed in its wines wherever the grapes are grown, and whatever style (dry, medium, sweet) is made. However, different soil types and different ripeness levels emphasise different aspects of this varietal character. Riesling has the ability, like Chardonnay, to express the nuances of individual vineyard sites and therefore it is common (especially in Germany, Alsace and Austria) for producers to bottle their wines with the name of the vineyard on the label.

12

THE FLAVOURS OF RIESLING

Riesling is an aromatic white grape variety. It is fruity and floral rather than herbaceous like Sauvignon Blanc. In cool climates, if the fruit is harvested when ripe (rather than over-ripe), the wines have green fruit flavours (green apple, grape) with floral notes and sometimes a hint of citrus fruit (lemon, lime). In moderate regions, citrus and stone fruit notes become dominant, and some wines can smell very strongly of fresh lime or white peach.

As a variety that slowly builds up sugars and retains its acidity well, Riesling is suitable for late-harvesting in regions where there are stable, dry, sunny autumn conditions. Stone fruit and tropical fruit notes can develop (peach, apricot, pineapple, mango). These late-harvest styles can be dry, medium or sweet in style. Riesling is very susceptible to noble rot, which concentrates sugars and acidity and makes this grape ideal for lusciously sweet wines (see Chapter 16).

High acidity levels and intense fruit help many Riesling wines to age in the bottle, where they develop flavours of honey and toast. Smoky petrol-like aromas sometimes appear in old Riesling wines. New oak is almost never used.

PREMIUM RIESLING REGIONS
Germany

Germany is the home of Riesling, producing wines in a wide range of styles. Basic Rieslings will be classified as *Qualitätswein*. These are usually light-bodied, dry, fruity and refreshing. This category includes many of Germany's best Rieslings. In addition, there is a *Prädikatswein* category, in which wines are categorised according to the sugar levels in the grapes. These vary in style according to their particular Prädikat. (German labelling terms are also explained in Chapter 4.)

Kabinett Rieslings are light in body, with high acidity and green fruit notes (apple, grape). They usually have medium sweetness and light alcohol, although they can be dry with medium alcohol.

Compared with *Kabinett* wines, **Spätlese** (late-harvest) Rieslings have a bit more body, with notes of citrus and exotic fruit (lemon, pineapple).

Auslese Rieslings have even more body and exotic fruit notes (pineapple, mango). This is the highest category to appear as a dry wine, although most Riesling *Auslese* wines are either medium or sweet.

Beerenauslese and **Trockenbeerenauslese** Rieslings are sweet wines made from noble rot affected grapes (see Chapter 16).

Eiswein is a sweet wine made from frozen grapes (see Chapter 16).

The region of **Mosel** produces Germany's lightest-bodied Rieslings. The *Kabinett* and *Spätlese* wines are almost always made with medium sweetness balanced by high acidity. The most prestigious vineyards are on very steep slopes surrounding the villages of Piesport and Bernkastel. **Rheingau** is a smaller region. Its *Kabinett*, *Spätlese* and *Auslese* Riesling wines are usually drier in style and medium-bodied. **Pfalz** is a large, southerly region that lies close to Alsace. The Riesling wines from vineyards around Forst and Deidesheim are generally off-dry and medium-bodied. The region with

the largest area under vines in Germany is the Rheinhessen, located to the north of Pfalz. Historically, the best vineyards are located on the west bank of the Rhine and produce some of the fullest-bodied German Rieslings. Today, quality wines come from a variety of sites.

France

In eastern France lies **Alsace**. Here the Vosges Mountains to the west shelter the region from rain-bearing winds blowing across northern France. Vines are planted on the eastern foothills, benefiting from the morning sun. The long, dry, warm autumns in Alsace provide ideal conditions for dry, medium-bodied Rieslings, with green, citrus and stone fruit notes. Fuller-bodied, late-harvest wines are also made, with more intense flavours and sometimes a hint of sweetness. Alsace has a very complicated geology, with a wide range of soil types.

The characteristics of Riesling wines can differ markedly from one site to another, even when the same winemaking techniques are used. The best wines benefit greatly from bottle age, and can last for decades, developing a smoky, honeyed complexity, often with petrol-like aromas.

The name of the grape variety usually appears on the label, along with the appellation. There are two appellations within Alsace: **Alsace AC** and **Alsace *Grand Cru* AC** (a wine from a superior vineyard site).

Austria

Austria also produces medium and full-bodied dry Rieslings with citrus and stone fruit flavours and medium or high acidity. Wines from certain vineyards can have smoky, mineral aromas, which can help the wines to gain complexity as they age.

Australia and New Zealand

Australia produces outstanding Rieslings, particularly in the **Clare Valley** and **Eden Valley** Regions. These are dry, medium-bodied, with high acidity and pronounced citrus fruit notes (lime, lemon). The wines age well, developing notes of honey and toast. Some wines rapidly develop smoky aromas that are similar to petrol. Sweet wines are also made with this grape.

New Zealand produces some very good quality Rieslings, mainly in the South Island. These can be dry or off-dry, with high acidity and intense green fruit and citrus flavours (apple, grape, lime). Most are best consumed young, but some develop attractive honey flavours with age.

Region of production. ⟶ ALSACE

APPELLATION ALSACE CONTRÔLÉE

HVH

DEPUIS 1639

Varietal labelling of AOC wines is common in Alsace but rare in the rest of France. ⟶ **RIESLING**

Producer. ⟶ "HUGEL"®

MIS EN BOUTEILLE PAR HUGEL ET FILS · RIQUEWIHR · FRANCE

PRODUCE OF FRANCE   BOTTLED IN FRANCE

LABELLING IN GERMANY

Prädikatswein must include one of the following terms on the label: **Kabinett**, **Spätlese**, **Auslese**, **Beerenauslese**, **Trockenbeerenauslese** and **Eiswein**. These terms are discussed in more detail in this chapter and in Chapter 16. Producers will have a range of these in their portfolio, and the labels can look very similar. Here are some examples from the Mosel producer Dr. Loosen.

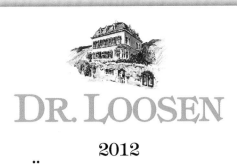

German labels also frequently include the name of the village and vineyard area from which the grapes come. In the examples above the village is Ürzig, and Würzgarten is an individual top-quality vineyard. However, the vineyard area can sometimes refer to a group of vineyards from a large area that includes many lesser-quality sites. There is a famous example of this from the village of Piesport. Piesporter Goldtröpfchen comes from the single vineyard of Goldtröpfchen, which towers steeply above Piesport (shown in the picture opposite). Piesporter Michelsberg, on the other hand, comes from a wide area including some sites that are several kilometres from Piesport. Unfortunately, there is no easy way to distinguish from the label whether the named site is a premium single vineyard or a large group of sites with lower-quality potential.

Grosses Gewächs (**Erstes Gewächs** in the Rheingau) indicates a high-quality dry wine made from riper grapes (equivalent to *Spätlese*, though these are classified as *Qualitätswein*). The grapes must come from one of the best individual named vineyards. Red wines are made from Pinot Noir (called Spätburgunder in Germany), and the best white wines are made from Riesling. It is important to remember that *Grosses Gewächs* is a private labelling system set up by the best German wine producers for their own use to indicate what they, and most independent observers, consider to be their top vineyard site.

Producer.

Vineyard name (not legally delimited).

Region: Clare Valley is one of the classic regions for premium Riesling in Australia and the world.

BULK-PRODUCTION REGIONS FOR INEXPENSIVE RIESLING

Riesling is not a variety that is widely associated with inexpensive bulk production. Most of the cheap, medium-sweet wines made in Germany are not made from Riesling. However, inexpensive fruity dry Rieslings are an important part of German production. Some Australian brands include a Riesling in their portfolio. Much of the fruit for these will be sourced from premium areas such as the Eden or Clare Valleys, rather than the hot bulk-production regions further inland. Volumes are small.

RIESLING IN BLENDS

For premium-quality wines, Riesling is almost never blended. Little, if any, Riesling is used in the large volume, inexpensive, medium-sweet German wines. In Australia, it is occasionally blended with the aromatic Gewurztraminer, to make fruity, off-dry whites.

A NOTE ON VARIETAL LABELLING

Almost all Riesling wines are varietally labelled. It is worth pointing out that there are other varieties that have similar names. The most commonly encountered one is Welschriesling/Laski Rizling/Olaszrizling. This is a totally unrelated variety, widely grown in central and eastern Europe for crisp, light-bodied dry whites and a few luscious sweet wines.

Other White Grape Varieties and White Wines

As well as the classic grape varieties there

13

are a number of other white grape varieties that have local importance within the country they are grown in. There are also a number of wines that are not recognised by their variety but rather by their geographical indication. This chapter will look at a range of local varieties and named wines from both Europe (France, Italy, Spain and Portugal) and New World countries (America, Australia, New Zealand and South Africa).

PINOT GRIS/PINOT GRIGIO

There are two names for the same grape variety: one is French and one is Italian. Producers outside France and Italy can use these names to indicate a particular style of wine.

The classic region for **Pinot Gris** in France is Alsace. Here the style is for full-bodied dry to off-dry, medium and sweet white wines with spicy tropical fruit flavours (ginger, banana, melon), sometimes with hints of honey. **New Zealand** Pinot Gris is a variety growing in popularity. It is made in a variety of styles, ranging from dry to sweet in the Alsatian model.

Pinot Grigio is grown throughout Italy. Typical Pinot Grigio is dry, medium or light in body, with medium acidity and a neutral character. Better examples, from Trentino-Alto Adige and Friuli-Venezia Giulia, show some of the ripe nuttiness and honeyed character for which this variety is prized in Alsace. Outside Italy, Pinot Grigio is typically used to describe wine that is neutral and medium to light-bodied in style.

VERDICCHIO AND TREBBIANO

In Italy, **Verdicchio** is a high-acid and medium-bodied white with flavours of lemon, fennel and bitter almond. Most is produced in the Marche and some of the best examples come from Verdicchio dei Castelli di Jesi DOC. Italy's most widely planted white grape variety is **Trebbiano**. With high levels of acidity, it is mainly used for inexpensive neutral white wines but occasionally it appears as a varietal wine.

ITALIAN NAMED WINES

In **Italy**, **Soave** and **Soave Classico DOC** are white wines from north-east Italy and made from Garganega, a late-ripening variety with floral notes (chamomile) and flavours of green fruit (pear, red apple) and white pepper. Most Soave is medium in body and unoaked. For information on the term *classico*, see Chapter 14. Far to the west in Piemonte, **Gavi DOCG** is a light, high-acid white made from Cortese. It has high acidity with notes of green apple and citrus.

Some of the vineyards of Domaine Schlumberger. The best vineyard sites of Alsace are always planted on steep east-facing slopes.

OTHER WHITE GRAPE VARIETIES AND WHITE WINES

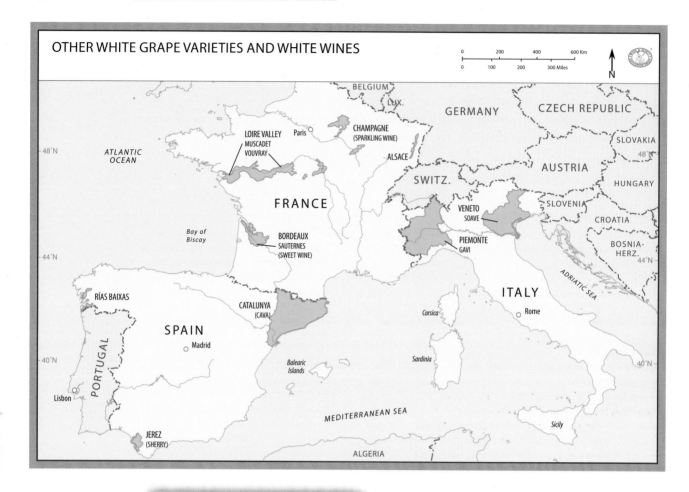

Brand.

Torrontés is a grape variety that has thrived in Argentina.

Region: Salta is a large region that includes Cafayate, which is a particularly celebrated area for the production of Torrontés.

CHENIN BLANC

In the cool-climate region of **Touraine** in the Loire Valley, the **Chenin Blanc** grape variety is used for white wines in a range of styles. Most are medium-bodied wines, with medium sweetness, high acidity, and are unoaked, with citrus, green and tropical fruit notes (lemon, apple, pineapple), and some herbaceous aromas (green leaf). Dry and sweet whites are also made. Chenin Blanc, like Riesling, Pinot Gris and Sémillon, is very susceptible to noble rot (see Chapter 16). The main appellation for Chenin Blanc is **Vouvray AC**, which produces wines in a variety of dry, medium and sweet styles.

   Chenin Blanc is widely grown in **South Africa**, mainly for large volume inexpensive white wines. Most of these are medium-bodied, dry or off-dry, with citrus and tropical fruit flavours. Despite the hot climate conditions, the wines have medium or even high acidity. Chenin Blanc is also used in blends (including Chenin Blanc-Chardonnay, where its role is similar to that of Semillon in Australian Semillon-Chardonnay blends) because it makes possible the production of large volumes at lower prices, and contributes some refreshing acidity and citrus fruit to the blend. Increasing amounts of premium-quality Chenin Blancs are now being made in South Africa, some of which have prominent oak flavours.

Chenin Blanc bush vines in South Africa.

MELON BLANC

Muscadet in the Loire Valley produces medium-bodied, dry, unoaked white wines made from **Melon Blanc**, a white grape variety. These wines are light, with almost neutral fruit and medium or high acidity. The main appellation is **Muscadet AC**. Muscadet Sèvre et Maine AC is a sub-region that produces superior wines. Some of the wines have the term *sur lie* on the label. This means the wine has been bottled from a vessel containing the dead yeast left over from fermentation. These give a little more body and complexity to the wine.

VIOGNIER

Viognier is a variety that produces soft, full-bodied and aromatic wines. The best examples can be found in the **Northern Rhône**, producing wines that are low in acidity and high in alcohol, with delicate fruit and floral aromas (peach, pear, apricot, violet) and spicy notes.

   Southern France has also shown an increase in Viognier production. The appeal of Viognier is such that modest plantings are also found in **Chile**, **Argentina**, **Australia** and **California**.

ALBARIÑO

Spain produces many interesting white wines. In **Rías Baixas**, the **Albariño** grape variety gives light to medium-bodied wines with fresh green and citrus fruit (apple, pear, grapefruit). These are typically unoaked, with refreshing high acidity.

SEMILLON/SÉMILLON

Sémillon is an important variety in Bordeaux, where it is commonly blended with Sauvignon Blanc to make dry wines (see Chapter 10) and used to make sweet wine (see Chapter 16). As a single varietal wine, its best expressions can be found in Australia and, in particular,

Producer.

In Alsace, *Grand Cru* refers to the best vineyard sites in the region. The vineyard name (in this case, Kitterlé) always appears on the label.

Producer.

Bold, simple and clear varietal labelling that is typical of many New World wine labels.

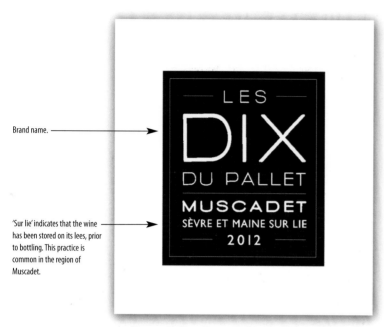

Brand name.

'Sur lie' indicates that the wine has been stored on its lees, prior to bottling. This practice is common in the region of Muscadet.

Semillon wines from other parts of Australia can range from medium-bodied simple citrus wines to wines that are intensely vegetal and pungent.

GEWURZTRAMINER

The classic home of **Gewurztraminer** is Alsace. Here the variety produces intensely perfumed white wines, that can be dry, off-dry or medium in style, and full-bodied, with high alcohol and low acidity. Typical flavours include floral perfume (rose, orange blossom), tropical and stone fruit (lychee, peach, grape), and musky sweet spices (ginger). Most are best consumed while they are youthful and freshly fruity, but some develop interesting honey and nut aromas with age.

Gewurztraminer is another Alsatian variety with an increasing reputation in **New Zealand**.

TORRONTÉS

Torrontés is a local speciality for **Argentinian** white wines. It is an aromatic variety, giving medium-bodied dry white wines with high alcohol, medium acidity, and pronounced fruity and floral aromas (perfume, grapes, peach). Like Malbec, it is widely grown, but most of the best examples come from the **Cafayate** region in the northern province of Salta.

the **Hunter Valley**. Hunter Valley Semillon is dry, light in body and alcohol, but high in acidity. It has delicate citrus aromas in youth, verging on neutrality. With age, it builds layers of complex toast, honey and nut flavours.

Other Black Grape Varieties and Red Wines

There are many other black grape varieties that have local importance within the country they are grown in. There are a number of wines that are not recognised by their variety but rather by their geographical indication. This chapter will look at a range of local varieties from both Europe (France, Italy, Spain and Portugal), as well as New World countries (America, Australia, New Zealand and South Africa).

14

Gamay vines in Beaujolais a few weeks after budburst.

GAMAY

Lying directly to the south of Burgundy sits the region of Beaujolais, which is home to the **Gamay** grape variety. Its moderate climate produces light and medium-bodied red wines with medium or high acidity and low tannin levels. These are usually unoaked, with pronounced red fruit aromas (strawberry, raspberry, cherry), sometimes with a hint of spice (cinnamon, pepper). They are best consumed while young and fruity, though some of the best wines from the Beaujolais Crus can improve with bottle-age.

TEMPRANILLO

The most important region for premium Spanish reds is **Rioja DOCa**. The main grape for this moderate-climate region is **Tempranillo**. This gives full or medium-bodied reds, with medium acidity, medium tannins and red fruit flavours (strawberry). It is often blended with Garnacha (Grenache), which can be the dominant variety in inexpensive Riojas. Grenache supplies high alcohol, and some spicy notes, with light tannins (see Chapter 11).

Much of the character of traditional-style Riojas comes from the oak ageing. This softens the tannins, and gives sweet coconut and vanilla flavours to the wine. Over time, some very savoury animal and vegetal flavours can develop (meat, leather, mushroom), particularly in the *Gran Reserva* wines.

Ribera del Duero DO also produces premium-quality red wines from Tempranillo, with black fruit notes (blackberry, plum), and toasty oak flavours. In **Navarra DO**, Tempranillo is often blended with international grape varieties such as Merlot and Cabernet Sauvignon.

Good-quality reds are made in a range of styles in **Catalunya**, using Tempranillo, Garnacha and international grape varieties.

Tempranillo and Garnacha are grown throughout Spain, and the oak-ageing techniques used in Rioja are widely adopted. There are many regions producing wine in a similar style to Rioja (soft tannins, strawberry fruit, oak flavours), but usually the hot growing conditions result in wines with less intensity or complexity.

DOURO

High-quality red wines are made in many Portuguese regions, but the **Douro DOC** has the most well-established

BEAUJOLAIS LABELLING TERMS

As in other parts of France, there is also an appellation hierarchy within the region of Beaujolais. At the bottom of the hierarchy is the generic appellations **Beaujolais AC** and **Beaujolais Nouveau AC** – the only difference being that wines labelled as *Beaujolais Nouveau* are a very light style of Beaujolais released in the November following the harvest. **Beaujolais Villages AC** is used to describe superior-quality wines that come from the granite hills to the north of the region. This group of villages accounts for about a quarter of the total production of the region. Within this region alone sits a small group of ten villages that are considered to make the best wines. They have all been awarded their own appellations. These are the **Beaujolais *Crus***. The most commonly seen ones are **Fleurie AC**, Brouilly AC, Morgon AC and Moulin-à-Vent AC.

reputation. This hot region also produces sweet, fortified Port (see Chapter 17), and its dry red wines are usually produced from Port grape varieties. There are several of these, and they are usually blended, but the best is Touriga Nacional, which is sometimes used on its own. Touriga Nacional gives low yields of wines that are deep in colour, high in acid and tannin, with intense flavours of dark berry fruits and spices (blackberry, blackcurrant, pepper, liquorice). The wines are usually aged in oak.

NEBBIOLO AND BARBERA

The most famous wines from **Italy's** Piemonte region are **Barolo DOCG** and **Barbaresco DOCG**. Both are made from **Nebbiolo**, which gives full-bodied wines with high tannins, alcohol and acidity. Red fruit flavours are

accompanied by floral and earthy elements that can evolve with age into complex aromas of tobacco, mushroom and tar.

Piemonte also produces wines from the **Barbera** variety. These have light to medium tannins and high acidity with aromas of red fruit and black pepper. Because of the moderate tannins, Barbera is often aged in oak, which adds flavours of toast, vanilla and sweet spice.

SANGIOVESE

One of Italy's most important red wines is **Chianti** (including **Chianti Classico**) **DOCG** from central Tuscany. Classic Chianti is dominated by the **Sangiovese** grape variety, although a small portion of other varieties can

---

SPANISH LABELLING TERMS: QUALITY AND STYLE

Throughout Spain, it has been traditional to age wines for long periods of time in oak barrels, and then in bottle before release. This means that at any time, the vintages being released by Spanish producers are often older than those from other countries, even for inexpensive wines.

In Spanish law there are labelling terms that indicate minimum periods of ageing in barrel and bottle. Although there are specified national requirements, some regions have stricter land laws, and in any case many producers exceed the basic requirements. Therefore, the most important thing to remember is the order they come in. In order of increasing age, they are:

- **Joven**. These wines are bottled the year following the vintage for immediate release, and indicate wines that have not been aged in oak for the minimum required time to be called *Crianza*.
- **Crianza**.
- **Reserva**.
- **Gran Reserva**. These wines are only produced in exceptional vintages. *Gran Reserva* reds can sometimes be quite pale and garnet in colour, and the best are very complex wines.

Many producers exceed the minimum ageing requirement for their quality wines. However, putting an inferior wine through the long ageing process results in wines that are tired, stale and lacking fruit. Nowadays, it is becoming more common to release wines after a shorter period of ageing while they are more youthful and fruity. For these young wines, some producers, like Cune, will not always choose to use the term *Joven* on their label. Instead, the only ageing terms they will choose to use will be *Crianza*, *Reserva* and *Gran Reserva*.

ITALIAN LABELLING TERMS: QUALITY AND STYLE

In addition to Italy's labelling terms (see Chapter 4), like Spain, there are other labelling terms that are widely used to describe a wine's quality and style. The two which are most widely seen are:

- **Classico**: indicates the historic centre of many DOC and DOCG regions, such as **Chianti Classico**. Often located on hills, these are usually the best sites and produce the best wines.
- **Riserva**: indicates that a DOC or DOCG wine has achieved a higher minimum level of alcohol and has been matured for at least a minimum number of months before release.

Castelgreve is a producer of a range of Chianti wines. Their labels are shown above. It is worth noting that producers within Chianti Classico will not necessarily produce a Chianti.

be added to the wine. Much basic Chianti is inexpensive and simple but better wines coming from sub-regions such as **Chianti Classico DOCG** are among Italy's finest. **Brunello di Montalcino DOCG** is made from 100 per cent Sangiovese, which produces medium to full-bodied reds with high levels of tannin and acidity necessary for long ageing. Flavours include plum, earth, red cherries and herbal notes (green tea).

OTHER LOCAL ITALIAN VARIETIES AND RED WINES

In north-east Italy, the main region for red wines is the Veneto, the home of **Valpolicella** and **Valpolicella Classico DOC**. These are both made from a blend of grapes, with Corvina dominating. The wines range considerably in style. Inexpensive wines typically have a light body, pale to medium ruby colour, low tannins and high acidity, with flavours of sour red cherry. More expensive examples from vineyards in the hills behind and west of Verona have more concentration and complexity, with flavours that hint at baked fruit, including plums, dried red cherries and prunes. **Amarone della Valpolicella DOCG** is a very complex full-bodied, dry wine with high tannins, made from grapes that have been partially dried to concentrate their flavours. Alcohol levels are among the highest in Italy.

Abruzzo is a region in east-central Italy famous for **Montepulciano d'Abruzzo DOC** made from the Montepulciano grape. Deep in colour, this wine has high

levels of acidity, and medium to high levels of tannin and alcohol with typical flavours of black cherry, blackberry and plums. Inexpensive examples are simple with jammy black fruit. (This wine should not be confused with Vino Nobile di Montepulciano DOCG, a Chianti-style red wine made from Sangiovese near the Tuscan town of Montepulciano.)

Southern Italy has long been famous for producing enormous volumes of red wine used for blending. Recent investment, however, has resulted in an increased number of high-quality wines. These are frequently a blend of local and international varieties, often labelled under the less stringent IGT regulations. Designations such as IGT Terre Siciliane allow both blending across a huge area and the grape variety(ies) to be clearly stated on the label. In Puglia, the most important black local varieties include **Primitivo** and Negroamaro, both of which produce wines that are medium in colour, acid and tannins with flavours of jammy black fruit and liquorice. Primitivo is the same variety as Zinfandel (see below). In Campania and Basilicata, the main black grape variety is **Aglianico**. This makes deeply coloured, intensely flavoured and full-bodied red wines with high levels of tannin and acidity, and complex floral and dark fruit aromas. Taurasi DOCG (Campania) is made from 100 per cent Aglianico. Its wines are full-bodied with complex floral and dark fruit aromas and high levels of tannin and acid.

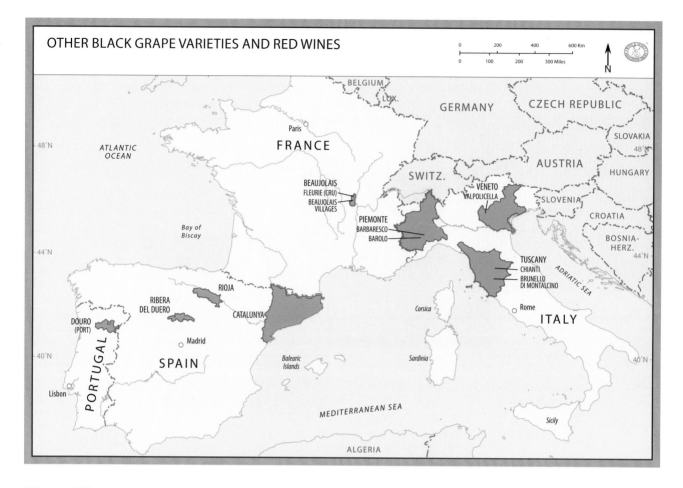

OTHER BLACK GRAPE VARIETIES AND RED WINES

In Mendoza, rainfall is very low. Here, Malbec vines are being supplied with water by flooding the vineyard.

ZINFANDEL

Zinfandel is a very important black grape variety for premium-quality wines in California. Although much is used for off-dry fruity rosés, commonly known as White Zinfandel, it shows its best in dry red wines. These wines are rich, full-bodied, and high in alcohol, with flavours of black fruit, dried fruit and sweet spices (blackberry, prune, raisin, clove, liquorice). The most intense, complex wines are made from old vines, with some Zinfandel vineyards planted over 100 years ago.

PINOTAGE

Pinotage is a black grape variety that was developed specially for the hot South African conditions. This variety is a close relative to the Pinot Noir grape variety, but prefers moderate or hot climates. Varietal Pinotage comes in a range of styles, but is typically full-bodied, with medium tannins and red fruit flavours (strawberry, raspberry, cherry), often accompanied by vegetal and animal notes (tar, leather).

CARMENÈRE

Carmenère is a very important black grape variety in Chile. It is originally a Bordeaux variety, which was introduced to Chile at the same time as Cabernet Sauvignon and Merlot. It is often used as a blend with these varieties. Varietal Carmenère wines are deep in colour, medium or full-bodied, with medium or high acidity and alcohol, and high levels of tannin. They have flavours of dark fruit (blackberry) and peppery spice. When underripe, Carmenère can show pungent green bell pepper and green bean flavours.

In order to ripen fully, Carmenère needs the warmest and sunniest sites, particularly those in the regions of Aconcagua and the Central Valley.

MALBEC

In Argentina, **Malbec** is the most important grape variety for premium red wines. This is originally a Bordeaux variety. It gives full-bodied wines with medium or high levels of tannin, which can make some Argentinian Malbecs suitable for ageing. The wines have a dark fruit character, often with spicy flavours (blackberry, black plum, clove, pepper), and the best wines benefit from oak ageing. It is common to blend Malbec with Cabernet Sauvignon and/or Merlot, but it is mostly seen as a single variety. It is grown widely in Argentina, but most plantings are in **Mendoza**.

Producer.

Malbec is a grape variety that has become closely associated with Argentina and, in particular, with the region of Mendoza.

15 Sparkling Wines

Nearly all quality sparkling wines are made using one of two methods: bottle-fermented and tank method. In both cases, the dissolved carbon dioxide that makes the wine fizzy is a by-product of a second alcoholic fermentation. Simply adding carbon dioxide is a third way of making sparkling wine. In the past, carbonation was closely associated with low-quality wine; however, this is no longer necessarily the case.

Both bottle-fermented and tank method sparkling wines start with a still base wine. This will usually be light in alcohol, because these processes add approximately 1–2% abv, as well as carbon dioxide (CO_2) gas dissolved under pressure.

BOTTLE-FERMENTATION METHODS

First, a still, dry **base wine** is produced and then blended with other wines. These can be from different vintages, varieties and/or villages. A mixture of sugar and yeast is added, before the wine is bottled, sealed and stored. A **second fermentation** then takes place, in which the wine increases slightly in alcohol, and the carbon dioxide, which cannot escape from the sealed bottle, becomes dissolved in the wine thereby creating the sparkle. During the fermentation process the dead yeast cells form a sediment in the bottle called 'lees'. This slow fermentation is followed by a period of ageing, during which the lees slowly releases flavours into the wine, a process called **yeast autolysis** ('self-digestion'). This is the most important part of the bottle-fermentation process, and accounts for many of the special flavours that appear in these wines (these flavours are described as *autolytic*). This process could last for a number of months, or even several years.

After ageing, the next stage is to **disgorge** (remove) the yeasty deposit, which otherwise makes the wine hazy.

In the **traditional method**, the bottle is slowly tipped and jiggled so that the yeast cells slide into the neck of the bottle. This tipping and jiggling can be done by hand (*riddling*) but is usually done mechanically, by machines (*gyropalettes*) that can process hundreds of bottles at a time. The plug of yeast in the neck is then frozen, and the pressure created inside the bottle by the CO_2 forces the plug out when the bottle is unsealed. The bottle is topped up with a mixture of wine and (usually) sugar. The amount of sugar added (the **dosage)** determines the sweetness of the final bottled product. Most wines made this way are '**Brut**', which means that a very small amount of sugar is used, but because of the high acidity of most sparkling wines, the wine tastes dry. *Demi-sec* or *semiseco* indicates medium sweetness.

An alternative method of removing the yeast is to empty the entire contents of the bottles into a tank under pressure. It is then filtered to remove the yeast, dosaged and rebottled. This **transfer method** is not permitted for Champagne or Cava, but it is common in New Zealand and Australia. It has the major advantage of being less labour-intensive, with little impact on quality.

These methods are much more labour-intensive than the tank method, and production costs are much higher. However, the main advantage in terms of quality is that through the extended contact they have with the dead yeast, the wines can gain complex bready, biscuity flavours that do not appear in other wines.

Bottle-fermented sparkling wines are widely perceived as better quality than other sparkling wines and therefore producers are keen to mention this production method on the label. Labelling terms such as 'traditional method', 'méthode traditionnelle' and 'bottle-fermented' are widely used. Note that if a label simply states 'bottle-fermented', it is likely that the transfer method, rather than the traditional method, was used.

Bottle-fermented Sparkling Wines

Champagne is the most famous traditional-method sparkling wine and is named after an AC region in northern France. The cool climate and chalky soils provide ideal conditions for base wines made from Pinot Noir, Meunier and Chardonnay that are high in acidity but with medium body and light alcohol. Because the region is so cool, and weather varies from vintage to vintage, the grapes do not ripen fully every year. To achieve quality and consistency, most wines are **Non-Vintage**, and the base wine is a blend of several vintages. In exceptional years, a portion of the best wine may be used to make a

Producer.

Brand name.
This is Moët et Chandon's
Prestige Cuvée, a premium-priced
luxury Champagne.

Unlike Non-Vintage,
Vintage is a term that appears
on Champagne labels.

The traditional way of moving the yeast deposit to the neck of the bottle is by hand. The bottles are placed horizontally in the A-frame (*pupitre*) and over a period of a few weeks are progressively raised to a vertical position.

Vintage Champagne. Due to high demand and limited supply, Champagne is never cheap. The least expensive Champagnes will generally see the minimum legal period of yeast autolysis (12 months), and can be made from the least-ripe grapes. They can be quite simple, with high acidity and green fruit flavours (green apple). Brands are very important in Champagne, ranging from BOBs (buyer's-own-brands) such as supermarket own labels, through co-operative-owned brands to the famous houses, known as *Grandes Marques*. Many of the best producers give their wines a long period of ageing before release. The better wines are typically dry, with high acidity, and complex flavours of green and citrus fruit (apple, lemon), and autolytic notes (biscuit, bread, toast). Vintage Champagnes are particularly complex wines, combining intense fruity and autolytic flavours with vegetal, nutty or honeyed complexity from bottle age.

Bottle-fermented sparkling wines are made in many other French regions. **Crémant** indicates a sparkling wine made using the traditional method. The major region for production is the Loire, particularly around **Saumur**, where Chenin Blanc is the main grape variety. These wines generally have high acidity and green and citrus fruit flavours, sometimes with some autolytic character, but they are rarely as complex as most Champagnes.

Cava is the Spanish term for traditional-method sparkling wines. The main grape varieties are local Spanish ones. The wines have fairly neutral fruit flavours (perhaps a hint of pear), medium acidity (less than Champagne), and very little autolytic complexity. Some houses use a portion of Chardonnay in the blend, which can give more complex wines. Most Cava is best consumed on release. The vast majority of Cava comes from Catalunya.

New Zealand, **Australia**, **South Africa** and **California** are important producers of bottle-fermented sparkling

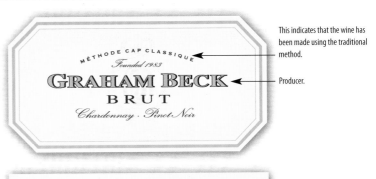

This indicates that the wine has been made using the traditional method.

Producer.

Producer.

Brut = dry. Most Champagnes are made in this style.
Note: this is a Non-Vintage (NV) wine. This does not appear on the label.

Producer: Freixenet is one of the two giant Cava producers. The other is Codorníu.

Método Tradicional is the Spanish term for Traditional Method. This states the Cava has been produced using the traditional method.

Brand name.

Most producers use the more efficient gyropalettes to move the yeast deposit to the neck of the bottle for the majority of their production.

wines. Both traditional and transfer methods are widely used. Brands are extremely important here, as in Cava and Champagne, and the variety of styles makes it impossible to generalise. The best wines use the Champagne grape varieties (Pinot Noir, Meunier and Chardonnay), and can be very intense and complex with long length.

Méthode Cap Classique is the term used in South Africa to describe sparkling wines made by the traditional method.

Sparkling Reds are a particular speciality in Australia. These are usually made with Shiraz and are full-bodied, with medium acidity and intense black and red berry fruit notes. Some are fruity and off-dry; others are dry, with leathery complexity from aged reserve wines. Premium examples are made using the traditional method but the tank method is also used.

TANK METHODS

This method begins in the same way as bottle-fermented wines. However, once the first fermentation is complete, the dry base wine is transferred to a pressurised tank, rather than a bottle. Sugar and yeast are added to start the second fermentation and the tank is sealed. This prevents any carbon dioxide gas from escaping, causing it to dissolve into the wine. Once the second ferment has finished, the wine must be filtered and bottled under pressure. This allows the carbon dioxide to be retained within the wine. These wines tend to have less lees contact than bottle-fermented sparkling wines, giving them little

or no autolytic character. When the bottle is opened, the dissolved carbon dioxide causes the wine to bubble.

This method is ideal for making fresh, fruity styles of sparkling wine such as Prosecco and Sekt. It is also widely used in the New World. Note that references to this method of production hardly ever appear on labels.

A variation on the tank method is used to make sweet sparkling wines with low levels of alcohol such as Asti. It is unusual because there is only one fermentation. Grape juice is placed in a pressurised tank and yeast is added to start the fermentation. Initially the carbon dioxide is allowed to escape. It is only towards the end of the fermentation that it is necessary to trap the carbon dioxide so that the right level of carbonation can be achieved. When the desired level of alcohol is reached the fermentation is interrupted by chilling the wine. The yeast is removed by filtration before the sweet sparkling wine is bottled under pressure.

Tank-fermented Sparkling Wines

Prosecco is a sparkling wine from north-east Italy. It is usually made using the tank method, although bottle-fermented versions also exist. The Glera grape variety gives a medium-bodied, dry or off-dry sparkling wine with delicate stone fruit flavours. Some are fully sparkling (*spumante*); others are just lightly sparkling (*frizzante*).

Asti DOCG is a sweet, fruity, light-bodied sparkling white from Piemonte in north-west Italy. It is made with the Muscat grape, which gives intense floral and fruity flavours (peach, grape, rose). It is usually fully sparkling, but wines labelled **Moscato d'Asti** just have a light sparkle and are generally lower in alcohol but higher in sugar content.

Sekt is simply the German word for sparkling wine. There are some very high-quality, bottle-fermented Sekts made in both Germany and Austria. However, most are simple, inexpensive tank-method wines. These can be medium or dry, and are generally light in body, with floral and fruity flavours. A wine labelled simply as **Sekt** will generally use cheap base wines sourced from anywhere within the EU. Deutscher Sekt can only be made from German base wines.

Tank-fermented sparkling wines are widely produced in the New World. One important new and very popular trend is the production of fully or lightly sparkling Moscato wines that are typically sweet and low in alcohol.

Sweet Wines

For almost all wines, red or white, the fermentation process continues until the yeast has converted all the sugar to alcohol and no detectable sugar remains. The resulting wines are dry. In order to make a sweet wine, three different methods can be used: the fermentation can be interrupted, a sweet component can be added to sweeten the wine, or, for some exceptional wines, the sugar levels in the grape juice are so high that sugar remains in the wine even after the yeasts are killed by the alcohol.

16

INTERRUPTING THE FERMENTATION

If the fermentation is stopped before the yeast has finished converting all the sugar to alcohol, the resulting wine will be sweet. This could be achieved by removing the yeasts using a fine filter to ensure that none remains in the liquid. Many of the off-dry and medium wines that are very popular with consumers are made this way. Alternatively, the yeast could be poisoned, using sulfur dioxide or alcohol. One common way to do this is to **fortify** (add alcohol) part way through the fermentation. This technique is used for Port as well as many fortified Muscat wines.

Sweet fortified Muscat wines are made widely around the Mediterranean from Greece to Portugal. They include *Vins Doux Naturels* such as **Muscat de Beaumes de Venise**, and Muscat de Rivesaltes from southern France. These are generally released unaged, and are best consumed soon after production while the intensely fruity aromas (grape, peach, perfume) are at their freshest. The wines are medium or full-bodied, and sweet, with high alcohol and medium or low acidity.

Sweet fortified Muscat wines are also made in other parts of the world, and are a particular speciality in Australia. Rutherglen Muscats, from a hot region in northern Victoria, are aged for a long period in oak. This causes the wine to oxidise and develop complex dried-fruit and kernel flavours (raisin, prune, fig, dried apricot, coffee, toffee). They are sweet and full-bodied, with high alcohol and medium or low acidity.

ADDING A SWEET COMPONENT TO THE BLEND

Adding sugar to wines to make them sweet is not permitted. However, some sweet liquids can be used for sweetening. These include the unfermented grape juice (*süssreserve*) used to sweeten some medium or sweet German wines. Apart from **Pedro Ximénez**, the traditional styles of **Sherry** (**Fino**, **Amontillado** and **Oloroso**) are dry. Sweet Pedro Ximénez Sherry, or mixes of grape juice and alcohol, or concentrated grape juice may be added to make Medium, Cream and Pale Cream Sherries.

CONCENTRATION OF SUGARS IN THE GRAPES

This group of methods is used for most of the greatest sweet wines. Yeasts die when the alcohol level reaches around 15% abv. If there is still some sugar left, then this will remain in the finished wine. The required sugar levels to achieve above 15% abv are not found in normally ripened grapes. However, there are ways of concentrating the sugar levels in the grape. One method is to **dry the grapes**. A variation on this method is to take advantage of **noble rot**. A third method is to **freeze the grapes**.

Dried Grape Wines

Drying the grapes causes them to shrivel. This could occur on the vine with some late-harvested grapes, or it can be done by laying the healthy harvested grapes out in well-ventilated, dry conditions to encourage evaporation. Sweet wines made this way include **Recioto** wines from Italy. An extreme example is **PX** (**Pedro Ximénez**) Sherry (see Chapter 17).

Noble Rot Wines

Noble rot, or *Botrytis cinerea*, is an important part of the production of many classic sweet wines, including **Sauternes**, **Tokaji**, Austrian and German **Auslese** (some), **Beerenauslese** (**BA**) and **Trockenbeerenauslese** (**TBA**) wines, and the sweet wines of the Loire. When *Botrytis cinerea* mould attacks healthy, ripe grapes, it weakens the

Separating Riesling grapes in Germany with Botrytis (noble rot) from those without. Depending on the level of rot, those in the small bucket may be used for *Beerenauslese* or *Trockenbeerenauslese*.

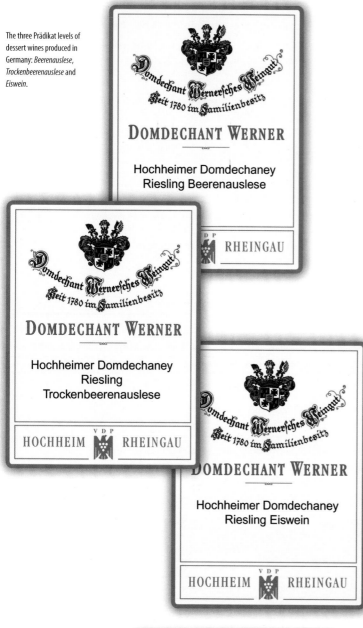

The three Prädikat levels of dessert wines produced in Germany: *Beerenauslese*, *Trockenbeerenauslese* and *Eiswein*.

Producer.

The best producers in Sauternes were classified into the same *Grand Cru* system in 1855 as the dry red wines of the Médoc.

Region of production.

skin, speeding up the evaporation of water from the flesh of the grapes and causing them to shrivel. As well as concentrating sugars and acids, the mould adds its own unique flavours to the wine. A combination of factors is needed to make these wines: a problem-free ripening period to ensure fully ripe, healthy grapes; damp, misty mornings to encourage the growth and spread of the botrytis mould; and warm dry afternoons to speed the drying out of the grapes. Such conditions are found in very few winegrowing regions, and cannot be relied on to occur every year.

The mould rarely affects all of the grapes evenly, which means that several passes may have to be made through the vineyard to pick all the grapes at the perfect stage of rottenness. Hand-picking is essential, and the laborious process of grape selection makes these wines expensive to produce. Where these wines sell at more modest prices, it is often because a less rigorous selection of grapes is used.

Certain grape varieties are particularly susceptible to noble rot, including **Riesling**, **Sémillon** and Chenin Blanc. The characteristic aromas of noble rot are hard to describe, and the best way to recognise them is to try a few examples of these wines. Descriptive terms that have been used include honey, dried apricot, ryebread, sweet biscuits, cabbage, orange marmalade, pineapple and mushroom.

Sauternes AC is a region located to the south of Graves AC in Bordeaux. Sémillon is the main grape variety, though Sauvignon Blanc is also used to add acidity and aromatic fruit flavours. Luscious sweetness is balanced by high acidity. These full-bodied wines have high alcohol and citrus stone fruit and botrytis flavours (lemon, peach), and often a hint of new oak (vanilla, toast, coffee). These wines age well, gaining honeyed complexity in the bottle.

Tokaji is a wine from north-eastern Hungary. Although some dry and medium wines are made, the most famous wines are the sweet Tokaji Aszú. These are classified with a number of *puttonyos* (ranging from three to six) that indicates the level of sweetness in the wine. The sweetest of these is six *puttonyos*, but even a three *puttonyos* wine is sweet. Tokaji wines are amber in colour, due to a long period of ageing in oak. They are full-bodied with medium alcohol and high acidity. They have intense flavours of dried fruits and sweet spices (orange peel, orange marmalade, dried apricots, raisins, cinnamon, ryebread). These wines age well, gaining notes of nut, coffee, caramel and honey.

Sweet and rare **Beerenauslese** (**BA**) wines and the even sweeter and rarer **Trockenbeerenauslese** (**TBA**) wines are *Prädikatswein* quality categories in Germany and Austria (see Chapters 4 and 12). In order to be classified as either a BA or a TBA, the levels of sugar in the must are required to be so high that they can normally only be achieved with the help of botrytis. These wines have low alcohol, medium body, and are very sweet with high acidity. Flavours depend on the

Producer.

Region and style. Aszú wines are the famous sweet wines of Tokaj.

This indicates the level of sweetness. A wine labelled *5 puttonyos* is very sweet.

grape variety used, but generally intense botrytis flavours are accompanied by dried fruit notes (dried apricot, raisin). In Germany, the finest BAs and TBAs are made with Riesling, generally from steep vineyard sites above the Rhine and Mosel.

Botrytis-affected sweet wines are also made in Coteaux du Layon AC, **Vouvray AC**, and other Loire appellations, from Chenin Blanc. In **Alsace AC**, botrytis-affected sweet wines are occasionally made from Riesling, Gewurztraminer, Pinot Gris or Muscat.

Australia produces good quantities of botrytis-affected sweet wines, mainly using Semillon or Riesling.

Frozen Grape Wines

In Canada, Germany and Austria, healthy grapes are sometimes left on the vine and harvested in winter while the water in them is frozen. The grapes are crushed while still frozen so that the ice crystals can be removed, leaving an intensely concentrated sugary grape syrup that is used to make sweet **Eiswein** (Germany and Austria) or **Icewine** (Canada). Because these are made with intensely concentrated juice from healthy grapes, the wines have very pure, pronounced, varietal-fruity flavours, high acidity, full body and syrupy sweetness. Riesling is the main grape used in Germany. These wines cannot be made everywhere and, depending on the location, are not always produced every year.

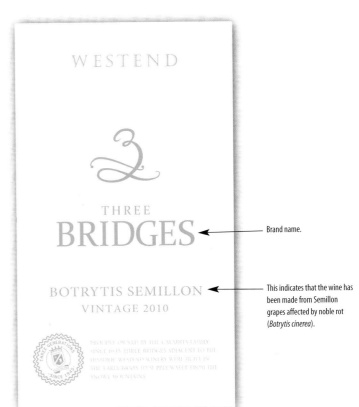

Brand name.

This indicates that the wine has been made from Semillon grapes affected by noble rot (*Botrytis cinerea*).

17 Sherry and Port

Sherry and Port are fortified wines, which means that additional alcohol is added to the wine. Sherry is a dry, medium or sweet fortified wine made around the town of Jerez de la Frontera in southern Spain. The base wine for nearly all Sherries is a neutral white wine, though after its special ageing process the final product can be amber or even deep brown in colour. Port is a sweet fortified wine made from grapes grown in the upper Douro in Portugal. Although white Port exists, most Port is purple, ruby or tawny in colour, depending on how it has been aged.

SHERRY PRODUCTION

There are many different styles of Sherry, but the starting point for almost all is a neutral, dry, low-acid white wine made from the Palomino grape variety. Fermentation usually takes place in stainless steel tanks. After it is complete, alcohol is added to fortify the wine before it goes through the *solera* ageing process.

Sherry is matured in old casks, called *butts*. These *butts* contain the wine but do not give it any oak flavours. Maturation takes place using the **solera system**. This is a technique that blends younger and older wines

Three of the classic styles of Sherry: *Amontillado, Oloroso* and *Pedro Ximénez*.

together continually as they age, ensuring a consistent style of mature wine. Most of the flavours in a Sherry come from this ageing process, and the differences in style between Sherries are due to differences in their ageing periods and conditions. After ageing, the Sherry can be sweetened.

SHERRY STYLES

Fino and Manzanilla Sherries are pale in colour, dry, medium-bodied, and typically with around 15% abv. The wine is kept fresh during the *solera* ageing process by a layer of yeast known as 'flor', which floats on the surface of the wine. This layer of flor protects the wine from air that would otherwise spoil it. It can only grow if the abv is around 15%. The yeast gives unusual bready notes to the wine, which has refreshing citrus zest and almond flavours. After bottling, these wines rapidly lose their freshness, so they should be chilled and consumed as quickly as possible.

Pale Cream Sherries are young Finos that have been sweetened with concentrated grape juice.

Amontillado Sherries are made by taking a Fino or Manzanilla, and adding more spirit to increase the alcohol and so kill off the flor. With no protection, the wine begins to oxidise. Amontillados have a deeper, amber colour and nutty flavours. When they are removed from the *solera*, Amontillados are dry wines and therefore wines simply labelled as 'Amontillado' will be dry. However, for some markets, it is common for them to be sweetened before bottling. These sweetened wines are labelled as Medium.

Oloroso Sherries are fortified after fermentation to 18% abv. At that strength, flor will not grow so oxygen attacks the Sherry throughout its ageing. The oxidation results in intense kernel and animal flavours (roasted nuts, coffee, meat). Oloroso wines are deep brown, and full-bodied with high alcohol. As with Amontillado Sherries, these are dry when they are drawn from the *solera*. All wines labelled Oloroso are dry, but it is common for the wine to be sweetened before bottling. These sweetened wines are labelled as **Cream** Sherries.

PX (**Pedro Ximénez**) are intensely sweet Sherries made from sun-dried Pedro Ximénez grapes. The wines are almost black, with intense dried fruit flavours (fig, prune, raisin, sultana). They are full-bodied, and syrupy in texture due to their extremely high sugar content. These are used as the sweetening component of the finest sweetened Sherries.

PORT PRODUCTION

Port is made from a blend of black grape varieties. The first step in the production process is to rapidly extract colour and tannins from the skins during a short period of fermentation. Then, whilst there is still a high proportion of sugar in the must, grape-derived spirit is added to the partly fermented grape juice. This kills off the yeasts, stopping the fermentation, and results in a wine that is sweet and high in alcohol. The wine is then aged in old oak vessels for a period of time before blending and bottling. It is this period of maturation that determines which style will be made.

PORT STYLES
Ruby Style Port

Ruby Ports are deeply coloured and fruity. They only spend a short period in large oak vessels and are bottled ready to drink. There are three main styles of Ruby Port.

Inexpensive **Ruby Port** is a non-vintage wine that generally undergoes less than three years' ageing before bottling. These are sweet, simple, fruity wines.

Reserve Ruby Port uses better quality wines, with more intense, complex fruit flavours. Longer cask ageing (up to five years) helps to soften and integrate the alcohol.

Late Bottled Vintage (LBV) Port is similar in style to a Reserve Ruby, but the wines come from a single year's harvest. Most of these wines do not need to be decanted. However, there are some that may not have been filtered before bottling, and will therefore have a deposit that requires decanting. 'Unfiltered' will appear on the label of these wines. All of these wines are ready to drink on release. Most show intense red and black fruit flavours (cherry, plum, blackberry), often with a hint of sweet spice (clove, pepper). They are sweet, with high alcohol, medium tannins and medium or low acidity.

Vintage Style Ports

Vintage Ports (including Single Quinta Vintage Ports) are very long-lived wines. The grapes come from the very best vineyards, and are only made in good years. They are bottled, unfiltered, after a short period in large oak vessels. Unlike Ruby and LBV Ports, these initially have high levels of tannin, as well as more intense fruit flavours. Although they can be enjoyed while still youthful, Vintage Ports benefit greatly from bottle age. The intense, spicy red and black fruit aromas of youth evolve into cooked fruit, animal and vegetal notes (prune, leather, wet leaves, coffee). As they age, these Ports leave a large deposit, so they *must* be decanted.

Tawny Style Ports

Inexpensive **Tawny Port** is a lighter style of Port, with toffee and caramel flavours. They are simply paler-coloured Ruby Ports, although some have their colour

adjusted by adding a little White Port (Port made from white grape varieties).

By contrast, **Reserve Tawny Ports** are made by ageing the wine for at least six years in small oak vessels. This breaks down the intense fruit flavours, and encourages oxidative, kernel flavours to develop (walnut, coffee, chocolate, caramel). Oxygen also attacks the colour, turning these wines medium tawny

Some *butts* from the Tio Pepe *solera* system in Jerez, which is made up of thousands of barrels.

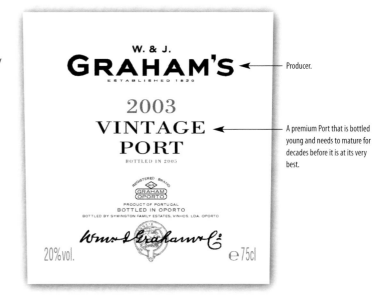

Producer.

A premium Port that is bottled young and needs to mature for decades before it is at its very best.

Steep terraced vineyards in the Douro Region in northern Portugal, where grapes are grown for Port production.

Producer.

A premium Port that is bottled after it has matured in wood barrels for 20 years and released ready to drink.

Ille terrarum mihi

TAYLOR'S®

praeter omnis angulus ridet, ubi vitus floret vinifera Hiberica. Ibi natum, et quercus ligneis va[...] ta[...]te mea conditum, per m[...]os [...] annos quiesco. Merum rubrum simplex ingredior: edenio

20

YEAR OLD TAWNY PORT
Aged for 20 years in wood

vinum involutissimum flavum Nunc est bibendum nunc vino pellite curras

ESTABLISHED IN 1692 • PRODUCT OF PORTUGAL
BOTTLED IN OPORTO BY
QUINTA AND VINEYARD BOTTLERS - VINHOS S.A.
VILA NOVA DE GAIA, PORTUGAL

20% VOL   **75 CL**

in appearance, rather than the opaque purple, ruby or garnet of Ruby and Vintage Ports. The very best of these are the **Tawny Ports with Indication of Age**, which could be labelled as **10**, **20**, **30** or **40** years old. The stated age is an average, not a minimum. These Ports do not need to be decanted because they do not form a deposit. They are best consumed as close to the bottling date as possible (this date is usually on the label). The best are exceptionally complex and concentrated, becoming tawny or even brown in colour with aromas and flavours of walnuts, coffee, chocolate, caramel and dried fruit. Where other styles of Port should be served at room temperature, Tawny Ports are best served slightly chilled.

Tasting and Evaluating Spirits

Tasting spirits is similar to tasting wines, although more emphasis is placed on the aromas and flavours, especially in the finish, and differences in the levels of sugar, acid and tannin are rarely important.

18

The ISO glass, used for evaluating wines, can also be used for spirits. Spirit tasting glasses have also been developed, with a similar shape but a smaller size.

If you are using an ISO glass, pour a 25 mL sample (half the volume you would use for wine). After describing the appearance, add 25 mL of water. This will help you assess the nose and palate without either of these being dominated by the alcohol.

Appearance

As with wines, we first need to assess the clarity of the spirit – in other words, what the spirit looks like. Like wine, spirits should be clear. Any cloudiness or haziness is usually a sign of a fault.

The colour of the spirit can give some indication of its style and age. Colourless spirits are often called 'White' and are generally unaged. However, some receive short ageing and their colour will have been removed before bottling by charcoal filtration. Golden and brown spirits usually have been aged in oak, although some can have their colour adjusted using caramel.

Nose

Nosing undiluted spirits will quickly cause your nose to dehydrate, and you will lose your sense of smell. For evaluating spirits, it is best to mix the spirit with an equal quantity of water. Adding the water will also help to release the aromas. The water should be at room temperature, and still mineral water is best. The amount you add must be the same for every sample so that a fair comparison can be made between the different spirits.

There is no need to swirl the spirit as you would a wine. This is because swirling will release alcohol, making it harder to assess the aromas of the spirit. Take quick, short sniffs only.

First, check the condition of the spirit. Cork taint is rare and spirits are more robust than wines, and less likely to be affected by poor storage. However, spirits that have been open for a long time lose their freshness because of their contact with the air.

Intensity should be assessed. All spirits, regardless of their colour, can range in intensity from neutral through to pronounced. The aroma groups for spirits are very different from those for wine, and generally reflect the base material, the ageing process or added flavours. Think about the aromas you can identify.

Palate

As with nosing, before tasting the spirit, it is a good idea to add some water to it. This will slow the onset of palate fatigue whilst also helping to open up some of the aromas.

Swirl the spirit around your mouth as you would with wine. Most spirits are dry, although some gain sweetness from the wood in which they are aged, or from added sugars. All spirits are high in alcohol. This can be detected as a warming and occasionally a burning sensation. So, instead, think about whether the alcohol is smooth and well integrated, or whether it seems harsh, compared with other spirits. Alcohol provides most of the viscosity and body of the spirit, although wood extracts and other flavour components can also contribute. Think about the body of the spirit: is it light, medium or full-bodied? Neutral style vodkas with smooth alcohol tend to be light in body, whereas pot still rums and peaty Scotch malt whiskies are full-bodied.

Generally speaking, the flavour characteristics on the palate should reflect those found on the nose. Classify the intensity of the flavours as light, medium or pronounced.

The biggest differences between spirits can be seen in the finish. Some spirits, such as neutral-style vodkas and rums, are made to have a short, clean, simple finish. Other spirits, especially Cognacs, whiskies and rums that have been aged for a number of years, can show a sequence of many different flavours for a period of a minute or more after you have spat or swallowed the sample.

Conclusions

As with wine, the factors that distinguish an outstanding spirit from an acceptable one are its balance, length, complexity, intensity and how well it expresses its category.

19   The Distillation Process

Distillation was originally used several centuries ago to produce medicines. Once people discovered the pleasurable effects of drinking distilled products, the use of distillation to produce strong alcoholic drinks became widespread. For the production of spirits, the alcoholic liquid goes through a process of distillation, the aim of which is to increase the alcohol content of the liquid.

In order to produce a spirit by distillation, it is necessary to start by using fermentation to make an alcoholic liquid. (The principles of the fermentation process are described in Chapter 3.) The aim of distillation is to separate the alcohol from the alcoholic liquid, most of which is water. When increasing the alcohol content of a liquid using distillation, advantage can be taken of the fact that ethanol (drinkable alcohol) boils at a lower temperature (78.3°C) than water (100°C). By heating an alcoholic liquid, the alcohol can be boiled off, and then collected, cooled and condensed back into a higher-strength alcoholic liquid. The water, which constitutes the largest proportion of fermented alcoholic liquids, is mostly left behind, along with any solids, colour compounds, sugars and most acids.

The equipment used for distillation is called a 'still'. There are many different kinds of still, but they can be divided into two broad categories: pot stills and column stills.

A Column Still

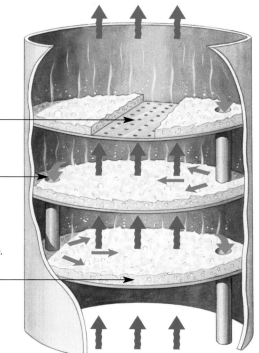

Vapours pass through the holes in the plate.

Less volatile parts, such as water, flow down the still as liquid.

On any given plate, the concentration of alcohol is higher than the one below but lower than the one above.

A layer of liquid forms on each plate.

Vapour entering the still.

POT STILLS

The **pot still** is the oldest, simplest kind of still. Pot distillation is a batch process. This means that once a distillation is completed, the still must be cleaned and refilled before the next distillation can begin.

The still consists of a pot-shaped vessel, usually made of copper, which contains the base alcoholic liquid. The alcoholic liquid is heated and this causes the alcohol to evaporate, turning it into a vapour. These vapours rise up the neck of the still, which extends above the pot like a chimney. Vapours in the neck then flow into a condenser, which uses cold water to condense them back into a liquid. This new liquid contains a higher level of alcohol than the original liquid. However, pot stills can only raise the level of alcohol in a liquid by a relatively small amount, so two or more successive distillations are needed to obtain a spirit of sufficient strength from an alcoholic liquid.

During the second distillation, the distiller only keeps part of the liquid that is collected from the condenser. The most volatile components, which boil off first, are called the **heads**. The **heart** (or spirit) follows second and contains the highest proportion of ethanol, and the lowest proportion of undesirable impurities. This is the part that is used to make the spirit. The least volatile components, known as the **tails**, boil off last. Heads and tails are not used in the final spirit because they contain concentrated levels of undesirable components. Instead, they are returned to the pot to be redistilled with the next batch because they still contain some desirable ethanol. Even with multiple distillations, the spirits produced are far from pure and retain a lot of character and flavour. (See the diagram opposite for more information regarding the workings of a pot still.)

COLUMN STILLS

A **column still** is so-called because of its arrangement in a tall, vertically structured column. The design is quite complex, and there are many variations.

However, all column stills are internally divided into a number of levels called 'plates'. These plates have holes to allow both the alcoholic liquid and vapour to easily move up and down the still. The alcoholic liquid is heated and enters the still as a vapour. Once operation is underway, the alcoholic vapour passes upwards through

A Pot Still in Cognac

This type of still can be seen *in situ* in Chapter 20.

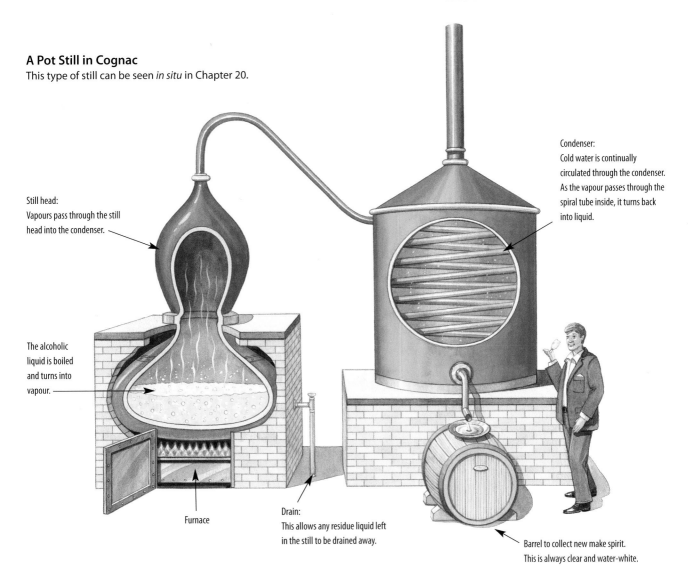

Still head:
Vapours pass through the still head into the condenser.

Condenser:
Cold water is continually circulated through the condenser. As the vapour passes through the spiral tube inside, it turns back into liquid.

The alcoholic liquid is boiled and turns into vapour.

Furnace

Drain:
This allows any residue liquid left in the still to be drained away.

Barrel to collect new make spirit. This is always clear and water-white.

---

the still. At each level some vapours will condense, forming a liquid layer on every plate. The rising vapours are forced through this layer of liquid causing it to boil, which, in turn, forces vapours upwards through the plate above. These mini-distillations take place on each plate, with the process continuing all the way up the still. With each distillation the concentration of alcohol increases. Therefore with a sufficient number of plates, a column still can produce a spirit that is almost pure ethanol. Such spirits are very smooth and light in character compared with those produced in a pot still. However, it is important to note that not all column stills are used to make such pure spirits.

Unlike a pot still, a column still can be run continuously and efficiently, meaning it is able to produce a constant flow of new spirit. This is why these stills are also known as 'continuous stills'.

INFLUENCE OF DISTILLATION STRENGTH ON FLAVOUR

There are various generalisations we can make when looking at the influences of distillation strength on the flavour of the spirit. As a general rule, spirits that are distilled to a lower alcoholic strength, like those produced using a pot still, contain more impurities and more flavour character, including that of the base material (barley, corn, apples, grapes, cherries, sugarcane, agave). However, these impurities also make the spirit harsher, so they generally need to be matured in oak or charcoal-filtered to soften them. Conversely, spirits distilled to a higher alcoholic strength, like those produced using a column still, are lighter in flavour and character. When reduced (watered down) to a standard bottling strength of around 40% abv, these spirits are relatively smooth, so they can be bottled and consumed without a period of maturation.

It is important to remember that it is the distillation strength, rather than the still type, that affects the flavour of the spirit the most.

POST DISTILLATION

Spirits can either be aged or unaged. Unaged spirits are stored in stainless steel tanks until they are bottled, normally shortly after distillation. Aged spirits are stored in oak vessels, typically barrels. The oak changes the colour and flavour of a spirit. Oak can soften out the harsh alcohol sometimes found in spirits that have just been distilled. It can also add oak flavours such as vanilla and sweet spice, and it allows oxygen to dissolve in the spirit over time to add an extra level of complexity.

Because sugar is non-volatile, all spirits are bone-dry when they come off the still. Any sweetness in the final bottled product is either added (e.g. with dark rums), or comes from the breakdown of oak into sugars during ageing (e.g. in Bourbon). The tannins and most acids that appear in fermented alcoholic drinks are also non-volatile, so they do not appear in the spirit. However, tannins can be absorbed from oak barrels during maturation.

All spirits are water-white when they come off the still. Any colour in the final spirit comes either from oak ageing or added colourings, such as caramel. Most aged spirits have their colour adjusted with caramel for consistency. Some short-aged spirits have all of their colour removed by filtering the spirit through charcoal – some white rums are treated this way.

Nearly all spirits have their alcohol level reduced before they are bottled and released for sale. De-mineralised water (used because it is neutral) is added slowly and mixed with the spirit to reduce it to an alcoholic strength suitable for bottling, typically around 40% abv.

Spirit Categories and Styles

There are many different spirit styles and categories available that vary from country to country. At each stage of the production process, the distiller can make choices that can affect the final flavours and style of a spirit, and, ultimately, which category the spirit ends up in. The flavour of a spirit depends on the type of raw material (fruit, grain, sugar cane), the type of distillation process (high strength and neutral, or low strength and characterful), and the maturation (if any) it receives after distillation (period of time in oak, type of oak).

20

BRANDY

Wine is made by fermenting whole, fresh grapes. If this is distilled, the product is brandy. Most brandy is aged in oak and/or coloured with caramel before bottling, so it is brown or amber in colour.

Cognac and Armagnac

Cognac is an oak-aged grape brandy from a delimited region to the north of Bordeaux. It *must* be double distilled using a copper pot still. The result is that Cognacs generally have distinctly fruity-floral aromas (grapes, perfume), and are medium to light in body, with smooth alcohol.

Armagnac is an oak-aged grape brandy that comes from a delimited area to the south of Bordeaux. Nearly all Armagnac is made using a version of the column still, which gives a relatively low-strength spirit that is full of character. Armagnac typically shows dried-fruit aromas (prune, raisin, fig) and is medium or full-bodied.

Oak maturation is an important part of the production of these spirits. This maturation makes the spirit smoother, and adds flavours of vanilla, toast, nuts, sweet spices, fruitcake and dried fruits. The labelling terms **VS**, **VSOP** and **XO** (**Napoléon**) are used to indicate the age of a spirit. The minimum ageing periods for these terms are set in law, although many companies age components of their blends for much longer than the legal minimum. Many other brandies use the same labelling terms but their usage is not controlled and they rarely have the same character or complexity.

WHISKIES

Whiskies are characterful oak-aged spirits made from grains such as barley, corn and rye. Unlike grapes, grains contain starch rather than sugar, and are solid rather than liquid. So, before fermentation can take place, the grains must go through a **conversion** process to turn the insoluble starch into fermentable sugars. This conversion occurs after the grains have been coarsely ground and mixed with hot water. However, for barley the process is slightly different. Before the starch can be converted into sugar, the barley grain is encouraged to germinate. Once growth is underway, the germination process is stopped by heating and drying the barley using a kiln. Peat is sometimes used as fuel in the kilning process, giving the final whisky smoky flavours characteristic of some Scotch

whiskies. The resulting grain, now called 'malted barley', is then mixed with hot water.

Once all the grains have had their starch converted to sugar, fermentation can begin, followed by distillation and maturation.

Scotch Whisky

Scotch Whisky *must* be both distilled and aged in oak casks in Scotland for at least three years. However, most are aged for much longer than this. An age statement on the bottle indicates the age of the youngest component.

Malt whisky is made using only malted barley, as described above. Distillation *must* take place in copper pot stills.

Barley.

A pair of pot stills in Cognac. The internal workings of this type of still are shown in Chapter 19.

A whisky warehouse in Scotland.

A **Single Malt Scotch Whisky** is a malt whisky that comes from just one distillery. Single malt whiskies vary greatly in style depending on how they are made. The level of peat used when kilning the barley, the type of cask used for maturation, and the length of maturation all have an impact on the flavour of the spirit. Because of these variations, it is impossible to generalise about styles. Peat can be a defining flavour but it is not always present. Other flavours may include floral, honey, fruity, dried fruit, nutty, medicinal, spicy, cereal and woody notes.

More detail about the typical regional styles of Highland, Islay, Campbeltown, Speyside and Lowland single malts can be found in the Glossary.

Grain whisky is a second kind of Scotch, which is made from a mixture of grains including corn, wheat, and malted barley. It is distilled in a column still, and produces a spirit that is smoother and lighter in flavour, compared with a Single Malt Whisky. Grain whisky is rarely seen on its own, but, instead, tends to be blended with malt whisky to create **Blended Scotch Whisky**. The quality and character of a blended whisky will depend on the characteristics of its component parts (malts and grains), and how well they are matched together. Some blended whiskies are intense in flavour; others are more delicate. Some have almost no peaty/smoky flavours; others are noticeably peaty. The best blended whiskies have a smooth spirit component and a well-balanced combination of flavours. Blended whisky is a very important whisky category, so each blend must be consistently produced year after year.

Irish Whiskey

Irish whiskies are generally made from a mixture of malted and unmalted barley, along with other grains, though there are some Irish malt whiskies. They are usually unpeated, though some use peat and are produced using pot stills and column stills or a combination of the two. Irish Whiskey tends to be much smoother and lighter in flavour than Scotch Whisky, with soft and mellow flavours of fruit, honey, flowers and oak.

North American Whiskies

Whiskey can be made anywhere in the USA, but Kentucky and Tennessee are two key states for whiskey production.

Bourbon is made using a mixture of grains, although by law it *must* contain a minimum of 51 per cent corn. Corn produces a spirit that seems sweeter than other grain-based spirits. The distillation process produces a relatively low-strength spirit with pronounced flavours. Much of the character comes from ageing the spirit in heavily charred new American oak barrels, which adds flavours of sweet coconut, vanilla, toffee and spice. Bourbon can be produced anywhere in the USA but the vast majority is produced and aged in Kentucky.

Tennessee whiskey can only be produced in the state of Tennessee. It is produced in a similar way to Bourbon. However, unlike Bourbon, the new make spirit is filtered through sugar maple charcoal before being put into barrel. This mellows the whiskey, resulting in a smoother spirit.

RUM

To be classified as a rum, the spirit *must* be made from a sugar cane product, of which molasses is most commonly used, producing rich rums, with flavours of toffee and ripe tropical fruit. Molasses, which is a thick syrupy substance, *must* be diluted with water before it can be fermented and then distilled. Distillation can occur in either pot or column stills, and as with other spirits, the distillation strength plays a major part in determining the style of the rum. After distillation, some rums can be aged in oak, adding flavours of spice, dried fruit, coconut and toffee. Colour can also be adjusted by the addition of caramel. It is common to divide rums into white, golden, spiced and dark rums.

White Rum

White rums are by far the most common style of rum and are a popular cocktail ingredient. The majority are distilled to a high strength, producing rums that are dry and neutral in character, rather like vodka. They are light in intensity, yet retain some characteristics from the raw material. Those distilled to a lower strength are very flavoursome, with very intense tropical fruit flavours. Note that white rums may have been aged in oak and then stripped of colour by charcoal filtration.

Golden and Spiced Rum

Golden rums are usually dry or off-dry, with smooth spirit due to a period of oak ageing. The better ones have intense, complex, fruity and oak aromas (banana, coconut, toffee). Spiced rums are typically golden rums that have spice flavourings added.

Dark Rum

Dark rums are generally full-bodied and sweet in style, with dried fruit and sweet spice flavours (fig, raisin, clove, cinnamon). Those that have most of their colour determined by added caramel may be harsh and spirity. The best are aged for several years in oak, and can be very smooth, intense and complex spirits.

TEQUILA

To be called Tequila, the spirit *must* be produced from 51 per cent blue agave in the delimited Tequila region in Mexico. The agave, a succulent and not a cactus, grows for around seven to ten years before being harvested at maturity for Tequila production. Once harvested, the outer leaves are removed and the hard core is cooked to create fermentable sugars. These sugars are then extracted, fermented and typically double pot distilled to make Tequila. Blue agave produces a spirit with distinct flavours of grass, citrus, earth and pepper, with sharp alcohol. As the spirit ages, the agave flavours mellow and are balanced by oak aromas of vanilla and sweet spice.

Tequila Styles

For many purists, **Blanco/Silver** Tequilas are the most authentic expression of an agave-based spirit. They are dry, with intense vegetable and spicy flavours (pepper). Many **Joven/Oro/Gold** Tequilas are simply unaged Tequilas that have had caramel added to alter the colour and soften the flavour. **Reposado** (rested) Tequilas are aged in oak for a short time, whereas **Añejo** (aged) Tequilas are aged for much longer than this.

VODKA

Vodka can be produced anywhere in the world. The classic raw materials used for the production of vodka are grains such as barley, wheat and rye, but other raw materials, including grapes and potatoes, can also be used.

By law, vodka must be distilled to a high strength of at least 95%–96% abv. This strength can only be achieved using a column still, although some producers will use pot stills during part of the production process. By distilling the spirit to such a high strength, little of the character of the base material remains. Many vodkas are filtered through charcoal to remove any remaining undesirable flavours and impurities. The final spirit is then reduced, by the addition of water, to a bottling strength of around 40% abv. They are typically unaged.

Vodka Styles

Most vodkas are made to be as neutral as possible. It is this light, neutral character that has made vodka such a popular and versatile spirit, ideal for cocktails and mixed drinks where the flavours of the other components are supposed to shine.

However, some vodkas are more characterful. These include many Polish and Russian vodkas, and some other

A harvest worker in Tequila who has cut away the leaves of an agave plant to reveal the hard core.

Molasses.

A column still used for vodka production. A large number of plates are required to make a 96% abv spirit. This can be seen in this picture, where each window in the column looks onto a different plate.

Some of the botanicals used in the production of Gin.

Angelica root

Coriander seeds

Juniper

Dried citrus peel

premium vodkas. The flavours of these are still delicate, compared with those of any whisky or brandy, but hints of the base material (grain, grape, potato) will show on the nose and the palate.

FLAVOURED SPIRITS

There are many spirits made by adding flavourings to a 95%–96% neutral base spirit. These include flavoured vodkas, and other categories such as gin and liqueurs. Flavourings can be added using the following techniques:

- **Maceration**, by soaking the flavouring ingredients in the spirit.
- **Re-distillation**, by re-distilling the spirit with the flavour ingredients.
- **Essences**, by adding artificial flavours to the spirit.

Flavoured Vodka

A range of flavoured vodkas are widely available. These are produced by adding extra flavourings, such as vanilla, fruit, toffee, herbs and spices, before bottling. Flavouring can be added either through the use of essences or by maceration.

Gin

Gin is a neutral base spirit that has been flavoured with ingredients called 'botanicals'. To be called gin, it *must* have juniper as the main flavouring. Other flavourings can be added, with the most commonly used being coriander seeds, angelica root and citrus peel.

By law, **London Dry Gin** *must* be produced by re-distilling the neutral spirit in a pot still with juniper and other botanicals. Once re-distillation is complete,

no other flavourings can be added. This creates a high-quality product, with intense and lasting flavours.

Distilled Gins are made in the same way as London Dry Gin except that other flavourings may be added after the re-distillation.

The production of **inexpensive gins** will see flavours added to the neutral spirit in the form of essences.

Gins are typically unaged.

Liqueurs

A liqueur is a distilled spirit that has been flavoured and sweetened. Most liqueurs are made using a neutral base spirit, but there are those which are based upon more flavoursome spirits such as brandy, rum or whisk(e)y. Flavouring is added to create different styles of liqueurs. The type of flavouring ingredients used can vary, but broadly speaking, they can be divided into four main categories: Dairy, Herb, Fruit and Seed/Nut. Many inexpensive liqueurs use artificial flavourings and colouring. This can make an enormous difference. For example, liqueurs made using real cherries or orange peel have a much more natural, genuine, persistent flavour than those using artificial flavours. This difference will be reflected in the price.

Before bottling, sugar is added. To be classified as a liqueur, the spirit is required by law to have a minimum level of sweetness. This level varies depending on where the spirit is made across the globe. Water is usually added to reduce the liqueur to a suitable alcoholic strength for bottling. Most liqueurs will then undergo some colouring. Artificial colourings are widely used as they give producers a broader range of colours to work with, and they help keep the final colour stable.

Glossary

The main text contains everything you will need to know to pass the WSET® Level 2 Award in Wines and Spirits Exam.
This Glossary is included as a reference resource to cover a number of other labels and production terms that are not part of the WSET® Level 2 Award in Wines and Spirits syllabus, but which you may encounter from time to time.

Abbreviations   **F** = French   **G** = German   **H** = Hungarian   **I** = Italian   **P** = Portuguese   **S** = Spanish
r = region   **w** = white grape variety   **b** = black grape variety

Acetic acid		The acid component of vinegar present in small quantities in all wines. Excessive amounts result in a vinegary nose and taste.
Adamado	**P**	Medium sweet.
Adega	**P**	Winery.
Agiorgitiko	**b**	Greek black variety (used in Nemea). Low in acidity, with soft tannins and rich, plummy fruit.
Alcohol		Potable alcohol, as contained in alcoholic drinks, is ethanol, sometimes called ethyl alcohol. Actual alcohol is the amount of ethanol present in a wine, measured as a percentage of the total volume at 20°C as shown on the label.
Aligoté	**w**	High-acid inexpensive dry white from Burgundy, usually unoaked. Will be varietally labelled to distinguish these wines from Chardonnay.
Almacenista	**S**	A producer of Sherry who ages it and then sells it in bulk to a merchant.
Alte Reben	**G**	Old vines.
Anbaugebiet	**G**	Designated quality wine region.
Appellation d'Origine Protégée	**F**	Protected Designation of Origin (q.v.).
Aragonez	**b**	Tempranillo, also called Tinta Roriz (in Portugal).
Assemblage	**F**	Blending of a number of different parcels of wine, particularly in Bordeaux or Champagne.
Assyrtiko	**w**	White variety with pronounced fruit and high acidity; the wines are usually dry and unoaked. From Greece, particularly Santorini. (Some sweet versions are also made, from dried grapes.)
Ausbruch	**G**	An Austrian quality category for sweet wines; the minimum must weight required is higher than that for *Beerenauslese*, but lower than that for *Trockenbeerenauslese*.
Azienda (or casa)	**I**	An estate that makes wine from both its own and bought-in grapes.
Azienda (or casa) agricola	**I**	An estate that uses only its own grapes in the production of its wine.
Azienda (or casa) vinicola	**I**	A producer who buys in and vinifies grapes.
Baga	**b**	High-acid, high-tannin Portuguese black grape, usually oak-aged. The main region is Bairrada.
Bandol	**r**	AC region in Provence, mainly making long-lived, full-bodied red wines from Mourvèdre (q.v.).
Bardolino	**r**	Red wine DOC region in north-east Italy; wines are similar in style to Valpolicella DOC.
Barrique	**F**	Cask (q.v.) with a capacity of 225 L. Traditional to Bordeaux, but now used throughout the world.

Barsac	**r**	AC region neighbouring Sauternes, making wines of a similar style, quality and price.
Bereich	**G**	A group of communes (*Gemeinde*).
Bergerac	**r**	AC region inland of Bordeaux, making wines in a similar style (red and white).
Bin		Literally a location (for example in a cellar), where a particular wine is stored. Often used as part of a brand name.
Biologique	**F**	Organic.
Blaufränkisch	**b**	Red cherry fruit and peppery spice. Oaked/unoaked. Austria (especially Burgenland) plus Germany and Hungary.
Blended whisk(e)y		Scotland: a blend of grain and malt whisky. USA: a blend of straight whiskey and neutral corn spirit.
Bodega	**S**	Winery.
Bonnezeaux	**r**	Loire AC region making sweet wines from noble-rot affected Chenin Blanc grapes.
Borderies	**r**	A region in Cognac, just north of Grande and Petite Champagne (q.v.), offering very high-quality spirits.
Botanicals		Flavourings used in gin production, such as juniper, coriander seeds and citrus peel.
Botrytis cinerea		Fungus that attacks the grape berry. In certain circumstances it will form unwanted grey rot; in others, desirable noble rot.
Bottiglia	**I**	Bottle.
Brut	**F, S**	Dry (of a sparkling wine).
Bull's Blood		Medium-bodied Hungarian red made from a blend of varieties, including Blaufränkisch and international varieties.
Bush vines		Vines trained as free-standing plants, not needing the support of a trellis.
Butt		Traditional barrel used in Sherry production, holding about 600 litres.
Cahors	**r**	AC region in south-west France, making full-bodied reds, mainly from Malbec.
Calvados	**r**	Delimited region in north-west France, making apple (and pear)-based aged spirits.
Campbeltown	**r**	Town on the west coast of mainland Scotland. Campbeltown single malt whiskies vary in style, but the best are very complex.
Cantina sociale	**I**	Co-operative cellar.
Cap Classique		A South African sparkling wine made using the traditional method (see Chapter 15).
Carbonic maceration		Fermentation of whole bunches of black grapes with the berries initially intact. The intracellular fermentation results in well-coloured, fruity red wines, with little tannin.

Carignan	**b**	High-acid, high-tannin black variety. Suits hot regions such as the south of France and North Africa.
Cascina	**I**	Farmhouse (has come to mean 'estate').
Cask		Wooden barrel, usually made of oak, used for fermentation, maturation and storage of wines. Traditional names and sizes vary from region to region.
Cask strength		Particularly of malt whiskies, a spirit that has not been reduced (watered down) to a bottling strength of around 40% abv. These generally will not be filtered and will be very high in alcohol: sometimes over 75% abv. See also Overproof.
Casta	**P**	Grape variety.
Cave	**F**	Cellar (often underground) or winemaking establishment.
Cave coopérative	**F**	Co-operative cellar.
Cépage	**F**	Grape variety.
Cerasuolo	**I**	Cherry pink.
Chai	**F**	Above-ground warehouse for storing wine, usually in barrels.
Chambolle-Musigny	**r**	Commune AC in the Côte de Nuits famous for Pinot Noir.
Chaptalisation		Must enrichment (adding sugar to the grape juice to increase potential alcohol) specifically using beet or cane, named after Comte Chaptal, the Napoleonic minister who advocated its use.
Château	**F**	Producer in Bordeaux, generally, but not always, with accompanying house.
Chaume	**r**	Loire AC region making sweet wines from noble-rot affected Chenin Blanc. The best part of this is Quarts de Chaume AC.
Chiaretto	**I**	Light or pale rosé.
Cinsault	**b**	Black variety with savoury, meaty flavours. Suits hot conditions such as the southern Rhône (where it is blended with Grenache, Syrah and Mourvèdre) and South Africa.
Climat	**F**	A vineyard site.
Clos	**F**	Historically, a walled vineyard, although the walls may no longer exist.
Colombard	**w**	White variety grown in south-west France for distillation, and for high-acid, appley dry whites.
Commune		A small wine-growing region, usually surrounding one village.
Condrieu	**r**	Northern Rhône AC region making complex, expensive, exotic dry and off-dry whites from Viognier (q.v.).
Consorzio	**I**	Producers' trade association, whose members' wines are identified by an individually designed neck-label.
Continentality		The difference between summer and winter temperatures.
Co-operative cellar		Winemaking (and sometimes bottling and marking) facilities that are jointly owned by a number of growers.
Cornas	**r**	Northern Rhône AC region making full-bodied reds from Syrah.
Cortese	**w**	Variety used in Northern Italy (especially Gavi) for high-acid, unoaked dry whites with green and citrus fruit (pear, lemon).
Corton	**r**	Grand Cru AC in the Côte de Beaune, making red (Pinot Noir) and white (Chardonnay) wines. Includes Corton-Charlemagne Grand Cru AC.
Corvina	**b**	The main variety used (along with Molinara and Rondinella) for Valpolicella. High-acid, medium tannin, and cherry and prune fruit.
Côte	**F**	Hillside.
Côte Chalonnaise	**r**	Burgundy district making wines with some of the style and quality of those from the Côte d'Or, but at lower prices. See also Givry, Mercurey, Montagny, Rully.
Coteau(x)	**F**	Slope(s).
Coteaux du Layon	**r**	Loire AC region making sweet wines from noble-rot affected Chenin Blanc grapes.
Cru	**F**	A single 'growth', generally of quality. It might be a village or a vineyard.
Cru Artisan	**F**	A rank of Bordeaux châteaux, below *Cru Bourgeois* (q.v.).
Cru Bourgeois	**F**	A rank of Bordeaux châteaux, below *Cru Classé* (q.v.).
Cru Classé	**F**	A classified growth, normally in Bordeaux.
Cuvée	**F**	A blend, which could be of different varieties, regions or vintages, or it could be of different barrels or vats from the same estate or vineyard.
Dégorgement	**F**	See disgorgement (q.v.).
Dégorgement tardive	**F**	A Champagne that has been disgorged after an exceptionally long period of yeast autolysis.
Demi-sec	**F**	Medium-dry.
Denominação de Origem Protegida (DOP)	**P**	Protected Designation of Origin.
Denominación de Origen Protegida (DOP)	**S**	Protected Designation of Origin.
Denominazione di Origine Protetta (DOP)	**I**	Protected Designation of Origin.
Disgorgement		Removal of the sediment from a bottle in traditional method sparkling wine production (*dégorgement*).
Dolcetto	**b**	Piemontese black variety with juicy black fruit, soft tannins and moderate acidity.
Domaine	**F**	Estate.
Dosage	**F**	Adjustment of the sugar level in sparkling wines by the addition of *liqueur d'expédition* (q.v.) after disgorgement (q.v.).
Eau-de-vie	**F**	Spirit distilled to a maximum of 96% abv: literally, 'water of life'.
Edelfäule	**G**	Noble rot.
Edes	**H**	Sweet.
Einzellage	**G**	Individual vineyard.
Elaborado (por)	**S**	Produced (by).
Elevé en fûts de chêne	**F**	Aged in oak barrels.
Embotellado (por)	**S**	Bottled (by).
En Primeur	**F**	Wines, especially from Bordeaux, that are sold before they are bottled.
Entre-Deux-Mers	**r**	AC region in Bordeaux making dry whites.
Erzeugerabfullung	**G**	Bottled by the producer.
Estate		A producer who makes wine from grapes grown on their property only.
Ethanol		See alcohol.
Extra-sec	**F**	Off-dry (sparkling wines).
Fattoria	**I**	Estate.

Federspiel	**G**	In the Wachau, a category lying in between Steinfeder and Smaragd (q.v.).
Fine Champagne	**r**	On a bottle of Cognac, indicates that the grapes used come exclusively from Grande Champagne and Petite Champagne (q.v.), with the majority coming from Grande Champagne.
Fining		Removal of matter in suspension in a wine by the addition of a fining agent such as bentonite, which acts as a coagulant. Occasionally animal products are used, making such wines unsuitable for vegetarians, although none of the fining agent remains in the wine.
Flor	**S**	Yeast growth that forms particularly on the surface of Fino and Manzanilla Sherries, giving them a distinctive taste and protecting them from oxidation.
Frizzante	**I**	Slightly sparkling.
Garganega	**w**	The dominant variety in the highest-quality Soave wines. Green fruit, crisp acidity, medium-body.
Garrafeira	**P**	A superior wine with additional ageing.
Geschützte Geografische Angabe	**G**	Protected Geographical Indication (q.v.).
Geschützte Ursprungsbezeichnung	**G**	Protected Designation of Origin (q.v.).
Gigondas	**r**	Southern Rhône AC region making Grenache-dominated wines, comparable in style and quality to Châteauneuf-du-Pape.
Givry	**r**	AC Commune in the Côte Chalonnaise, making red (Pinot Noir) and white (Chardonnay) wines.
Grains nobles (sélection de…)	**F**	Botrytis-affected grapes (wine made using a selection of nobly rotten grapes). This is a legal description in Alsace, but the phrase may occasionally be seen on wines from other regions, such as Condrieu, Coteaux du Layon and Mâcon.
Grande Champagne	**r**	The quality centre of the Cognac region; a source of particularly elegant, complex spirits that age well in oak. See also Petite Champagne, Fine Champagne, Borderies.
Granvas	**S**	Tank-fermented sparkling wine.
Grechetto	**w**	Medium to high-acid white variety that is used for the best Orvieto DOC wines. Suitable for dry and medium (amabile) styles.
Grenache Blanc	**w**	White-skinned version of Grenache, used in southern France and northern Spain for full-bodied peachy whites with medium to low acidity.
Grosslage	**G**	A group of adjoining vineyards. Not to be confused with Einzellage.
Grüner Veltliner	**w**	High-quality grape variety grown in Austria. Styles range from light-bodied and refreshing to powerful and complex.
Highland	**r**	Scottish region, north of a line from Greenock to Dundee. Malt whiskies from this region are generally very intensely flavoured. See also Campbeltown, Islay, Lowland, Speyside.
Imbottigliato all'origine	**I**	Estate-bottled.
Indicação Geográfica Protegida (IGP)	**P**	Protected Geographical Indication (q.v.).
Indicación Geográfica Protegida (IGP)	**S**	Protected Geographical Indication (q.v.).
Indication Géographique Protégée (IGP)	**F**	Protected Geographical Indication (q.v.).
Indicazione Geografica Protetta (IGP)	**I**	Protected Geographical Indication (q.v.).
Invecchiato	**I**	Aged.
Islay	**r**	Island off the west coast of Scotland. Islay malt whiskies are generally very peaty, with seaweed, medicinal and brine aromas. See also Campbeltown, Highland, Lowland, Speyside.
Jumilla	**r**	Hot region in south-east Spain, making dark-coloured, full-bodied reds mainly from Monastrell (Mourvèdre).
Lambrusco	**b**	Traditionally a fruity, dry (or off-dry) sparkling red from Italy, made from the Lambrusco grape variety. Much exported Lambrusco is a sweet, lightly-sparkling white that is light in alcohol.
Lees		The sediment of dead yeast cells that gathers at the bottom of the tank or cask once fermentation is completed.
Lees stirring		A process of mixing the lees (q.v.) with the wine, usually in cask, to help extract components that will give the wine extra flavour and body.
Lieu Dit	**F**	A named vineyard site not of Premier Cru or Grand Cru status.
Liqueur d'expédition	**F**	A liquid mixture of wine and sugar, added to all bottle-fermented sparkling wines after disgorgement and before final corking. See dosage (q.v.).
Liqueur de tirage	**F**	Mixture of wine, sugar and yeast added to still wine to promote a secondary fermentation in sparkling wine production.
Liquoroso	**I**	Strong, often fortified, wine.
Lowland	**r**	Scottish region, south of the line from Greenock to Dundee. Lowland malt whiskies are generally light and smooth, with floral, grassy and cereal aromas. See also Campbeltown, Highland, Islay, Lowland, Speyside.
Maceration		Period of time when the skins are in contact with the juice or wine during red wine vinification.
Madeira	**r**	Aged, fortified wine from the island of Madeira. Comes in dry, medium and sweet styles. Grape varieties are named on premium and vintage versions: Sercial (dry), Verdelho (off-dry), Boal (Sweet), Malmsey (very sweet).
Madiran	**r**	AC region in southwest France, making full-bodied reds, mainly from Tannat (q.v.).
Malolactic fermentation		Conversion of harsh malic acid into softer lactic acid by the action of lactic bacteria. As a side effect, buttery, nutty flavour compounds can be produced.
Malt		Barley that has undergone the malting process of soaking, germination and kilning to convert the starch present in the original grain into fermentable sugar.
Malvasia	**w**	Fruity, aromatic grape variety used for the sweetest Madeiras (Malmsey), and some non-fortified sweet wines. Also used for the finest Frascati and white Rioja, although Trebbiano and Viura are more common.
Manipulant	**F**	A grape-grower who also makes wine, especially in Champagne.
Marc	**F**	1. The residue of skins, pips and stalks left in a press after the extraction of juice or wine. In English, this is called pomace. 2. Brandy made from this, rather than whole grapes.
Marsanne	**w**	Delicately flavoured, low-acid grape variety used for many full-bodied dry white Rhône wines, including white Hermitage AC. Often blended with Roussanne.
Mas	**F**	Vineyard.
Maso, Masseria	**I**	Estate.
Mataro	**b**	Mourvèdre (q.v.), especially in Australia.

Menetou-Salon	**r**	Loire AC region making Sancerre-style white wines from Sauvignon Blanc, and some light reds from Pinot Noir.
Merchant		1. A company that buys grapes or finished wine for vinification, maturation and blending before sale. 2. A wine dealer.
Mercurey	**r**	Region in the Côte Chalonnaise, best known for reds (Pinot Noir).
Metodo charmat	**I**	Tank method sparkling wine.
Metodo classico, Metodo tradizionale	**I**	Traditional method, bottle-fermented sparkling wine.
Mezcal		General category for Agave-based spirits. Tequila is a Mezcal from a delimited region.
Micro-climate		The climate within the canopy of the vine.
Millésime	**F**	Vintage date.
Mise en bouteille (par)	**F**	Bottled (by).
Mise en bouteille au château/domaine	**F**	Château/domain-bottled.
Mise sur lie	**F**	Bottled directly from the lees (q.v.).
Mistelle, Mistela	**F, S**	A mixture of unfermented grape juice and alcohol, such as Pineau des Charentes, Ratafia and most Moscatel de Valencia.
Moelleux	**F**	Medium-sweet.
Monastrell	**b**	Mourvèdre (q.v.), especially in Spain.
Monbazillac	**r**	Appellation within the Bergerac region (q.v.) making Sauternes-style sweet wines, mainly from Sémillon.
Monopole	**F**	A vineyard, especially in Burgundy, that has only one owner.
Montagny	**r**	Côte Chalonnaise region making white wines from Chardonnay.
Morey-Saint-Denis	**r**	AC Commune in the Côte de Nuits, best known for red (Pinot Noir).
Mourvèdre	**b**	Hot climate variety making deep-coloured, high-tannin, full-bodied spicy reds. Appears as part of the blend in southern Rhône, and alone in Bandol.
Mousseux	**F**	Sparkling.
Muffa nobile	**I**	Noble rot.
Must		Unfermented grape juice, destined to become wine.
Naoussa	**r**	Region in northern Greece making high-acid, high-tannin reds from Xinomavro.
Négociant	**F**	Merchant (q.v.).
Negroamaro	**b**	Southern Italian black variety. Literally 'black-bitter'. Used in Salice Salentino.
Nemea	**r**	Greek region making full-bodied soft fruity reds from Agiorgitiko.
Nero d'Avola	**b**	Sicilian black grape variety, used for full-bodied reds.
Non-filtré	**F**	Unfiltered.
Overproof		Most commonly used of Rum. Any spirit that is higher in alcohol than proof spirit (q.v.).
Palo Cortado		Dry style of Sherry that has similar flavours to Amontillado, but is more full-bodied.
Passito	**I**	A generally strong, sweet wine made from partially dried grapes.
Pétillant	**F**	Lightly sparkling.

Petit château	**F**	In Bordeaux, one of the many château brands that fall outside the classifications.
Petite Champagne	**r**	The Cognac region surrounding Grande Champagne (q.v.). Spirits made from Petite Champagne grapes are very high quality, but not quite as elegant, complex and ageworthy as those from Grande Champagne. See also Fine Champagne.
Pinot Blanc/ Pinot Bianco	**w**	White variety grown in Alsace and Northern Italy. Similar in flavour to Chardonnay, but usually unoaked or very lightly oaked.
Pipe		Traditional cask (q.v.) used in the Douro for Port production. Two sizes are recognised: the 550 L production, or Douro, pipe and the 534 L shipping pipe.
Podere	**I**	A small estate.
Pourriture noble	**F**	Noble rot.
Prädikat	**G**	The various sub-categories of *Prädikatswein* wines (*Kabinett*, *Spätlese*, *Auslese*, *Beerenauslese*, *Trockenbeerenauslese*, as well as *Eiswein*). Austria adds the category *Ausbruch*, but does not include *Kabinett*.
Primary aromas		Aromas in a wine that arise directly from the fruit (q.v. secondary, tertiary).
Produttore	**I**	Producer.
Proof		Of spirits, 57.1% abv (UK), 50% abv (USA). See also overproof.
Propriétaire	**F**	Owner.
Protected Denomination of Origin (PDO)		The EU sub-category of wine with Geographical Indication (q.v.) that sets the strictest requirements for wine production.
Protected Geographical Indication (PGI)		The EU sub-category of wine with Geographical Indication (q.v.) that allows the greatest flexibility to wine producers.
Pupitre	**F**	Rack consisting of two hinged boards through which holes have been bored to hold the necks of sparkling wine bottles during riddling (q.v.).
Puttonyos		Measure of sweetness in a Tokaji wine.
Quinta	**P**	Farm or estate.
Racking		Drawing off clear wine from a cask or vat and moving it to another, leaving the sediment behind.
Raisin	**F**	Grape.
Recioto	**I**	Similar to passito (q.v.), made with part-dried grapes.
Récoltant	**F**	Someone who harvests their own grapes.
Remuage	**F**	Riddling (q.v.).
Reserve		May indicate a superior quality wine, or wines that have seen a period of ageing. Or it may indicate very little. Unlike the word *Reserva* or *Riserva* in Spain, Portugal or Italy, this word has no legal meaning.
Residual sugar		Unfermented sugar remaining in the wine after bottling. Even dry wines will contain a small amount.
Reuilly	**r**	AC Loire region making Sancerre-style white wines from Sauvignon Blanc, and some light reds from Pinot Noir.
Ribatejo	**r**	Portuguese region, making red and white wines.
Rich	**F**	Sweet (sparkling wines).
Riddling		Moving the sediment to the neck of the bottle before disgorgement (q.v.) in traditional method sparkling wine production.
Roussanne	**w**	High-quality white Rhône variety. Usually blended (with Marsanne in the northern Rhône; with other varieties in the south). Full-bodied, medium to high acidity, orchard fruit flavours.

Ruby Cabernet	**b**	NOT Cabernet Sauvignon (although it is related). A variety created especially for very hot conditions such as Central Valley, California. Mainly used for simple, soft, fruity reds.
Rueda	**r**	DO region west of Ribera del Duero, making crisp, unoaked, fruity dry white wines from Verdejo and Sauvignon Blanc.
Rully	**r**	Côte Chalonnaise (q.v.) region, best known for white wines (Chardonnay) and sparkling wines.
Sainte-Croix-du-Mont	**r**	Region facing Sauternes across the River Garonne, making wines in a similar style but at lower prices.
Saint-Estèphe	**r**	Commune in the Haut-Médoc.
Saint-Joseph	**r**	Region in the northern Rhône, mainly making red wines from Syrah.
Saint-Julien	**r**	Commune in the Haut-Médoc.
Salice Salentino	**r**	DOC region in southern Italy, making full-bodied red wines mainly from Negroamaro (q.v.).
Savennières	**r**	AC region in the Loire, making complex, long-lived dry white wines from Chenin Blanc.
Secondary aromas		Aromas in a wine that arise from the fermentation (q.v. primary, tertiary aromas).
Single cask		Particularly of malt whiskies, a spirit that is not a blend of several casks. These are often bottled unfiltered, at cask strength (q.v.).
Site climate		The climate of a plot of vines, perhaps a vineyard, or part of a vineyard.
Smaragd	**G**	In the Wachau (Austria), rich, full-bodied dry wines from late-harvested grapes.
Solera		System of fractional blending used in the production of Sherry, wherein older wine is refreshed by the addition of younger wine.
Speyside	**r**	Scottish region, within the Highlands (q.v.). Speyside malt whiskies are generally very elegant, and well-balanced, with subtle peat and complex fruit, floral and honey aromas. See also Campbeltown, Islay, Lowland.
Spumante	**I**	Sparkling wine made by any method.
Steinfeder	**G**	In the Wachau (Austria), the lightest bodied wine category for dry wines.
Straight whiskey		USA: a whiskey made from at least 51 per cent of one grain, distilled to no more than 80% abv, and aged for a minimum of two years in new oak casks.
Strohwein, Schilfwein	**G**	Sweet wine made from grapes that have been dried on straw or reed mats.
Sulfur dioxide (SO_2)		Highly reactive and pungent gas that is used in winemaking as an anti-oxidant and antiseptic (additive E220).
Supérieur	**F**	Indicates a higher degree of alcohol.
Super Second		Bordeaux châteaux that were second (or third) growths in the 1855 Classification, but which sometimes produce wines that rival the first growths for quality. Which châteaux qualify is a matter of debate.
Sur pointe	**F**	Ageing of a bottle of sparkling wine, neck down, after yeast autolysis is complete, but before disgorgement.
Szamorodni	**H**	'As it comes'. Wine made from grapes that have not been sorted according to their degree of botrytis.
Száraz	**H**	Dry.
Tannat	**b**	High-tannin black grape variety grown in south-west France (especially Madiran AC), also popular in Uruguay. Often blended with Merlot.
Tarrango	**b**	Grape variety developed for hot conditions, used for light-bodied, Beaujolais-style reds, mainly in Australia.

Tavel	**r**	Southern Rhône AC specialising in full-bodied dry Grenache-based rosés.
Tenuta	**I**	Estate.
Terroir	**F**	A sense of place expressed in a wine, which may include the effects of climate, site climate, soils, aspect, slope, and even local grape varieties, yeast cultures and winemaking practices.
Tertiary aromas		Aromas in a wine that are due to the effects of ageing (q.v. primary, secondary aromas).
Toro	**r**	DO region in Spain, neighbouring Rueda (q.v.), making intensely fruity red wines, mainly from Tempranillo.
Tri (pl. Tries)	**F**	A selection of grapes, especially those grapes picked during one passage through a vineyard, selected at the perfect level of ripeness for sweet wines.
Trincadeira	**b**	Portuguese black variety, used for soft, plummy reds.
Uva	**I, S**	Grape.
Uvaggio	**I**	Blend of grapes.
Vacqueras	**r**	Southern Rhône AC region, making wines comparable in quality and style to Châteauneuf-du-Pape.
Vecchio	**I**	Old. For DOC wines there are controls as to how this word may be used.
Vendange	**F**	The wine harvest.
Vendange à la main	**F**	Hand-harvested.
Vendange Tardive, VT	**F**	Late-harvest. A wine made with exceptionally ripe grapes.
Verdejo	**w**	High-quality white fruity-aromatic grape variety, used for unoaked dry whites in Rueda (q.v.).
Verdelho	**w**	White grape variety used for fortified wines (especially in Madeira), for fruity dry whites.
Verdicchio	**w**	High-acid white grape variety grown in the Marche (especially Verdicchio dei Castelli di Jesi).
Vernaccia	**w**	High-acid white grape variety grown in Tuscany (especially Vernaccia di San Gimignano).
Vieilles vignes	**F**	Old vines. Not a legally defined term. Old vines give lower yields of generally higher quality grapes.
Viejo	**S**	Old.
Vigna, Vigneto	**I**	Vineyard.
Vignoble	**F**	Vineyard.
Viña	**S**	Vineyard.
Vin de paille	**F**	Wine made from grapes that have been dried.
Vine/grape variety		One of a number of recognisable members of a particular vine species. They may result from natural mutation or deliberate crossing.
Vine species		Any of the members of the genus *Vitis*. Most wine is made from European species, *Vitis vinifera*, but using American rootstocks from the species *V. rupestris* or *V. riparia*.
Vinha	**P**	A plot of vines.
Vinification		Winemaking.
Vino generoso	**S**	Fortified wine.
Vino Nobile di Montepulciano	**r**	Region in Tuscany making Chianti-style red wines from Sangiovese.
Vino novello	**I**	New wine, bottled shortly after the harvest.
Viognier	**w**	High-quality white grape variety, originally from the northern Rhône (Condrieu). Now grown more widely in southern France and New World countries. Gives exotically

scented (nashi-pear, white peach, violet, minerals), full-bodied, dry and off-dry wines.

Viticoltore, vignaiolo	I	Grower.
Viticulture		Grape growing.
Vitigno	I	Grape variety.
Viura	w	Spanish white variety, used for white Rioja and (along with Parellada and Xarel-lo) Cava. Also known as Maccabeo.
Vivace	I	'Lively'. Slightly sparkling.
Volatile acidity		Acetic acid (q.v.) in a wine. A small amount exists in all wines and is an important part of the aroma or bouquet. Excessive amounts indicate a faulty wine.
Volnay	r	AC Commune in the Côte de Beaune, specialising in red wines (Pinot Noir).
VOS, VORS		*Vinum Optimum Signatum, Vinum Optimum Rare Signatum.* These are age classifications for very old Sherries. VOS indicates an average age of at least 20 years; VORS indicates an average age of at least 30 years.
Vosne-Romanée	r	AC Commune in the Côte de Nuits, specialising in red wines (Pinot Noir). Includes Romanée-Conti *Grand Cru AC*.

Vougeot	r	AC Commune in the Côte de Nuits, specialising in red wines (Pinot Noir). Includes Clos de Vougeot *Grand Cru*.
Wine with Geographical Indication		A legal category of wines in the EU. This is subdivided into Protected Denomination of Origin (PDO) and Protected Geographical Indication (PGI).
Winzergenossen-schaft	G	Co-operative cellar.
Xinomavro	b	High-acid, high-tannin Greek grape variety (sometimes compared with Nebbiolo). Used in several Northern Greek regions, including Naoussa.
Yeast		Generic term for a number of single-celled micro-organisms that produce zymase, the enzyme responsible for converting sugar into alcohol. The most important wine yeast is *Saccharomyces cerevisiae*.
Yeast autolysis		Breakdown of dead yeast cells after the secondary fermentation in sparkling wine production. Among other things, it gives the wine a yeasty, or biscuity, nose.
Yecla	r	Hot DO region in south-east Spain, making dark-coloured, full-bodied reds mainly from Monastrell (Mourvèdre).

Index

World Wine Regions Map

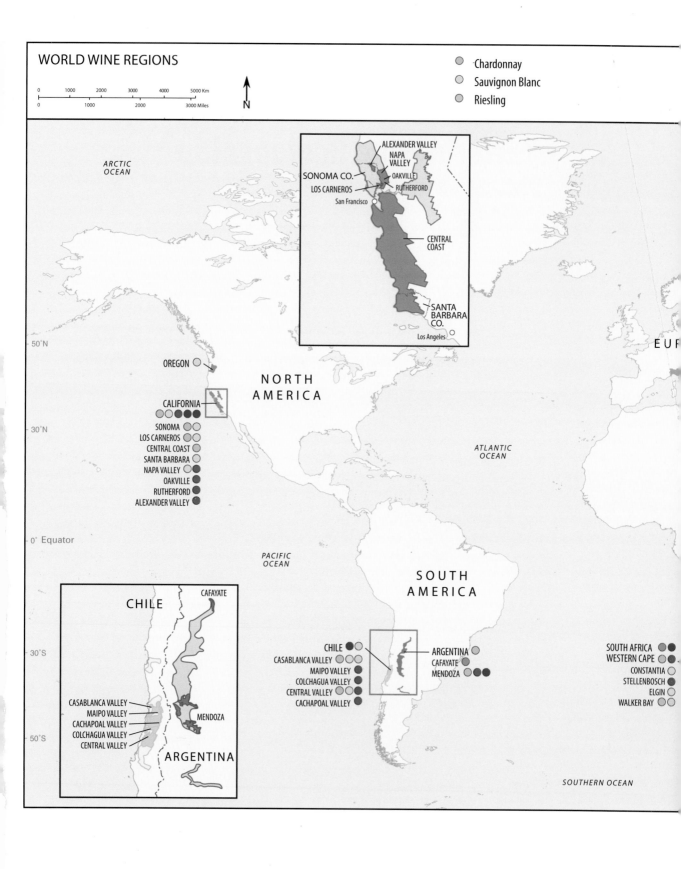

WORLD WINE REGIONS

| Chardonnay |
| Sauvignon Blanc |
| Riesling |

0   1000   2000   3000   4000   5000 Km
0   1000   2000   3000 Miles

N

ARCTIC OCEAN

ALEXANDER VALLEY
NAPA VALLEY
SONOMA CO.
LOS CARNEROS
OAKVILLE
RUTHERFORD
San Francisco

CENTRAL COAST

SANTA BARBARA CO.
Los Angeles

50°N

OREGON

NORTH AMERICA

CALIFORNIA
SONOMA
LOS CARNEROS
CENTRAL COAST
SANTA BARBARA
NAPA VALLEY
OAKVILLE
RUTHERFORD
ALEXANDER VALLEY

30°N

ATLANTIC OCEAN

0° Equator

PACIFIC OCEAN

SOUTH AMERICA

CAFAYATE

CHILE

30°S

CHILE
CASABLANCA VALLEY
MAIPO VALLEY
COLCHAGUA VALLEY
CENTRAL VALLEY
CACHAPOAL VALLEY

ARGENTINA
CAFAYATE
MENDOZA

SOUTH AFRICA
WESTERN CAPE
CONSTANTIA
STELLENBOSCH
ELGIN
WALKER BAY

CASABLANCA VALLEY
MAIPO VALLEY
CACHAPOAL VALLEY
COLCHAGUA VALLEY
CENTRAL VALLEY

MENDOZA

50°S

ARGENTINA

EUR

SOUTHERN OCEAN

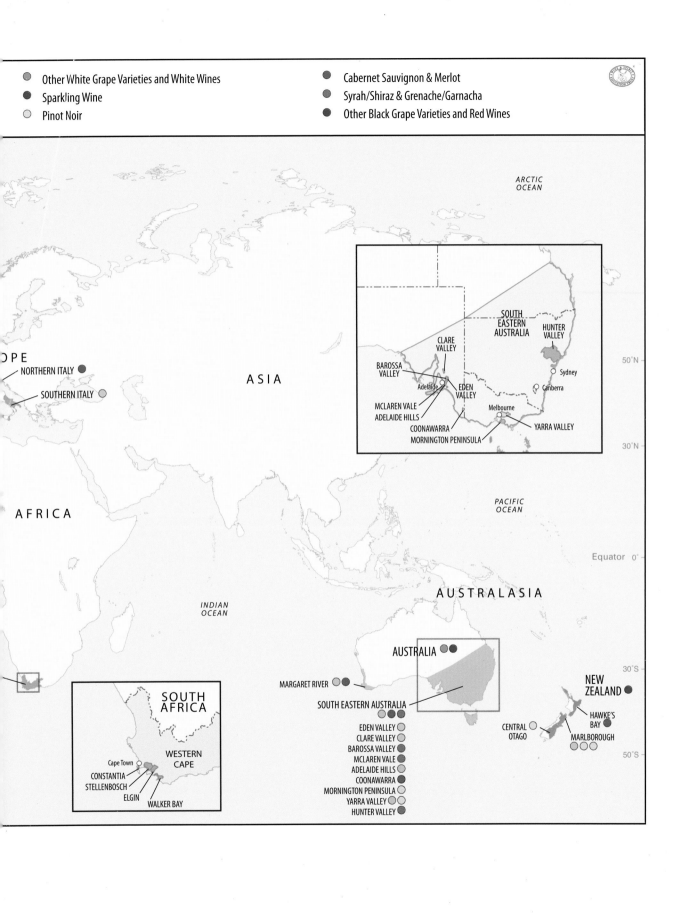

Legend

- Other White Grape Varieties and White Wines
- Sparkling Wine
- Pinot Noir
- Cabernet Sauvignon & Merlot
- Syrah/Shiraz & Grenache/Garnacha
- Other Black Grape Varieties and Red Wines

ARCTIC OCEAN

OPE

NORTHERN ITALY

SOUTHERN ITALY

ASIA

SOUTH EASTERN AUSTRALIA

CLARE VALLEY

BAROSSA VALLEY

HUNTER VALLEY

Adelaide

EDEN VALLEY

Sydney

MCLAREN VALE

ADELAIDE HILLS

Canberra

COONAWARRA

Melbourne

MORNINGTON PENINSULA

YARRA VALLEY

50°N

30°N

AFRICA

PACIFIC OCEAN

Equator 0°

INDIAN OCEAN

AUSTRALASIA

AUSTRALIA

30°S

MARGARET RIVER

NEW ZEALAND

SOUTH EASTERN AUSTRALIA

HAWKE'S BAY

EDEN VALLEY

CENTRAL OTAGO

CLARE VALLEY

BAROSSA VALLEY

MARLBOROUGH

MCLAREN VALE

50°S

ADELAIDE HILLS

COONAWARRA

MORNINGTON PENINSULA

YARRA VALLEY

HUNTER VALLEY

SOUTH AFRICA

WESTERN CAPE

Cape Town

CONSTANTIA

STELLENBOSCH

ELGIN

WALKER BAY